45291

£2 50

THE OPEN UNIVERSITY

Mathematics: A Third Level Course

Complex Analysis   Units 8 and 9

Singularities
Cauchy's Theorem II

D1438328

Prepared by the Course Team

The Open University Press

The Open University Press, Walton Hall, Milton Keynes.

First published 1975

Produced in Great Britain by
Technical Filmsetters Europe Limited, 76 Great Bridgewater Street, Manchester M1 5JY

ISBN 0 335 05552 4

This text forms part of the correspondence element of an Open University Third Level Course. The complete list of units in the course is given at the end of this text.

For general availability of supporting material referred to in this text, please write to the Director of Marketing, The Open University, P.O. Box 81, Milton Keynes, MK7 6AT.

Further information on Open University courses may be obtained from The Admissions Office, The Open University, P.O. Box 48, Milton Keynes, MK7 6AB.

CONTENTS

Unit 8 Singularities

Unit 9 Cauchy's Theorem II

Unit 8   Singularities

Conventions

Before working through this text make sure you have read *A Guide to the Course: Complex Analysis.*

References to units of other Open University courses in mathematics take the form:

Unit M100 13, Integration II.

The set book for the course M231, Analysis, is M. Spivak, *Calculus*, paperback edition (W. A. Benjamin/Addison-Wesley, 1973). This is referred to as:

Spivak.

Optional Material

This course has been designed so that it is possible to make minor changes to the content in the light of experience. You should therefore consult the supplementary material to discover which sections of the text are not part of the course in the current academic year.

8.0 INTRODUCTION

So far in the course we have been concentrating on the properties which follow from the fact that a function is analytic on a region, but in this unit we shall examine functions which fail to be analytic at certain points of a region. In spite of their bad behaviour at such points certain functions can still be analysed by the methods that we have developed. For example, we show that it is possible to expand some functions as a Laurent Series (generalization of Taylor Series), even though the functions might fail to be analytic at a point of the region under consideration.

There is much in this unit of a theoretical nature, and indeed it forms a crucial step in our progress towards the important Residue Theorem of *Unit 10, The Calculus of Residues*, but this theory supports some important techniques of calculation, particularly of calculating integrals (though it will not be very obvious to begin with how this is relevant). You should put a lot of effort into the problems, which are there to help you develop these techniques. In particular, do not skimp on Section 8.9, which is a mixed bag of problems intended to give you an opportunity to revise almost all of the techniques developed in the course so far.

Television and Radio

In the fifth television programme we begin a line of investigation into the evaluation of contour integrals by indirect methods, which will be continued in this and the next two units. The programme contains a discussion of the proof of one of the main theorems of this unit, the theorem on Laurent series. It is designed as an introduction to the unit.

The fourth radio programme deals with a collection of problems on the classification of singularities of functions.

8.1 SINGULARITIES

We begin with some examples.

Consider these three functions:

$$z \longrightarrow \frac{\sin z}{z}, \qquad z \neq 0;$$

$$z \longrightarrow \frac{\cos z}{z}, \qquad z \neq 0;$$

$$z \longrightarrow \exp\frac{1}{z}, \qquad z \neq 0.$$

Each has for domain the region $\mathbf{C} - \{0\}$ (the complex plane with the exception of the point 0); each is analytic on its domain. But none of them is defined at 0. We say that 0 is a *singularity* of each of these functions. (We shall give the precise definition after we have discussed these three examples.)

If we examine the function $z \longrightarrow (\sin z)/z$ more closely, we soon come to the conclusion that there is not much wrong with it at 0. In the first place, $\lim_{z \to 0} (\sin z)/z$ exists, and is equal to 1. So the function

$$z \longrightarrow \begin{cases} \dfrac{\sin z}{z}, & z \neq 0 \\ \\ 1, & z = 0 \end{cases}$$

is continuous at 0. But we can do better than that: by Theorem 10 of *Unit 6, Taylor Series*, $\sin z = z + z^3 g(z)$, where g is entire; therefore $(\sin z)/z = 1 + z^2 g(z)$ for $z \neq 0$. The function $z \longrightarrow 1 + z^2 g(z)$ takes the value 1 at 0, so it is equal to

$$z \longrightarrow \begin{cases} \dfrac{\sin z}{z}, & z \neq 0 \\ \\ 1, & z = 0. \end{cases}$$

Since g is entire, we conclude that

$$z \longrightarrow \begin{cases} \dfrac{\sin z}{z}, & z \neq 0 \\ \\ 1, & z = 0 \end{cases}$$

is analytic everywhere (including 0). So by defining a suitable value for the function at 0, we have been able to remove the singularity. Accordingly, we describe the point 0 as a *removable singularity* of the function $z \longrightarrow (\sin z)/z$.

The singularities of $z \longrightarrow (\cos z)/z$ and $z \longrightarrow \exp 1/z$ at 0 are not removable. If a function f has a singularity at 0, a necessary condition for the singularity to be removable is that $\lim_{z \to 0} f(z)$ exists (so that we may give a value to the function at 0 which makes it continuous, at least). Neither $\lim_{z \to 0} (\cos z)/z$ nor $\lim_{z \to 0} \exp 1/z$ exists. In fact, since $\cos$ is continuous at 0 and $\cos 0 = 1$, there is a disc with centre 0 on which $|\cos z| > \frac{1}{2}$, say, and so by taking $|z|$ sufficiently small we can make $|(\cos z)/z|$ larger than any given positive number. This means that $z \longrightarrow (\cos z)/z$ cannot approach any limit near 0. To show that $z \longrightarrow \exp 1/z$ does not have a limit near 0, we argue as follows. Since $\lim_{x \to \infty} e^x = \infty$, we have $\lim_{x \to 0^+} e^{1/x} = \infty$. Thus $z \longrightarrow \exp 1/z$ is not bounded on any disc centre 0, and so cannot have a limit there.

It is clear enough that what is wrong with the function $z \longrightarrow (\cos z)/z$ is that $\cos 0 \neq 0$. If we take any function g, which is analytic on a neighbourhood of zero and such that $g(0) \neq 0$, then the function $z \longrightarrow g(z)/z$ will have a singularity at 0 which will not be removable. More, generally, the function $z \longrightarrow g(z)/z^m$, where m is a positive integer, will have a non-removable singularity at 0. A function of this form is said to have a *pole* at 0. So $z \longrightarrow (\cos z)/z$ is an example of a function which has a pole at 0.

Singularities which are poles do not look too frightening, since they are constructed in such an obvious way. But removable singularities and poles do not exhaust all the possible kinds of singularity. The singularity of the function $z \longrightarrow \exp 1/z$ is not a pole, as we now show. If the singularity were a pole, we would be able to write $\exp 1/z = g(z)/z^m$, for $z \neq 0$, where, in this case, g is entire, $g(0) \neq 0$ and m is a positive integer. But then we would have $g(z) = z^m \exp 1/z$, $z \neq 0$, and since $\lim_{z \to 0} g(z)$ would exist, it would have to be true that $\lim_{z \to 0} z^m \exp 1/z$ existed. In fact this limit does not exist. One of the properties of the real function $x \longrightarrow e^x$ is that for any positive integer, m, $\lim_{x \to \infty} e^x/x^m = \infty$. (See Theorem 17-6 of **Spivak**.) It follows that $\lim_{x \to 0^+} x^m e^{1/x} = \infty$. The function $z \longrightarrow z^m \exp 1/z$ cannot be bounded on any disc centred at 0, and so cannot have a limit near 0.

A singularity which is not removable and is not a pole is called an *essential singularity*. The singularity of the function $z \longrightarrow \exp 1/z$ at 0 is an essential singularity.

We have shown that the three functions we began with all have singularities at 0, but these singularities are of different types. The singularity of $z \longrightarrow (\sin z)/z$ is removable, that of $z \longrightarrow (\cos z)/z$ is a pole, and that of $z \longrightarrow \exp 1/z$ is an essential singularity.

It is time to turn from particular examples to generalities, and to set out some definitions.

Definition

Suppose that the function f is analytic on some punctured disc $0 < |z - \alpha| < r$, but not on the open disc $|z - \alpha| < r$. Then α is called a **singularity** of f. (Note that f does not have to be defined at α.)

If f has a singularity at α, but there is a complex number a such that the function

$$z \longrightarrow \begin{cases} f(z), & z \neq \alpha \\ a, & z = \alpha \end{cases}$$

is analytic on a neighbourhood of α, then α is said to be a **removable singularity**, and we **remove the singularity** by setting $f(\alpha) = a$.

If f has a singularity at α, and there is a function g, analytic on some neighbourhood of α, with $g(\alpha) \neq 0$, and a positive integer m such that $f(z) = \dfrac{g(z)}{(z - \alpha)^m}$ for $z \neq \alpha$, then α is said to be a **pole** of f.

We call m the **order of the pole**, and say that f has a pole of order m at α.

A pole of order 1 is often called a **simple** pole.

A singularity which is neither a removable singularity nor a pole is called an **essential singularity**.

That looks like rather a lot of definitions, but the only term we have not mentioned before is the order of a pole. The function $z \longrightarrow (\cos z)/z$ has a pole of order 1, or simple pole, at 0.

There are a few points worth making about our definitions.

Our examples were chosen for simplicity as well as for being typical; do not be misled by them into thinking that singularities occur only at 0, or that a function can have only one singularity.

In most practical cases a function is given by a rule, or formula; we look for singularities of the function among those points where the rule breaks down. But in order to qualify as a singularity, a point at which the rule breaks down must be surrounded by a punctured disc on which the function is analytic. Thus the singularities of a rational function are just the zeros of the denominator. On the other hand, the function $z \longrightarrow \operatorname{cosec} 1/z$ fails to make sense when $z = 0$ or $1/(n\pi)$, where n is a non-zero integer. (By cosec we just mean the function $1/\sin$, of course.) The points $1/(n\pi)$ are singularities, but there is no punctured disc $0 < |z| < r$ on which the function is analytic, so 0 is *not* a singularity. It is something rather more nasty, and we do not intend to discuss such points in this unit.

The requirement in the definition of "singularity at α" that the function f be analytic on a punctured disc $0 < |z - \alpha| < r$ is not intended to preclude the possibility that it be analytic on a larger punctured region. It is a minimum requirement. All the examples at the beginning of this section are analytic on the punctured plane $\mathbf{C} - \{0\}$, for instance. In particular, they are all analytic on the punctured disc $0 < |z| < 1$. But it is sometimes convenient to think of the punctured plane as a "punctured disc of infinite radius"—which means to say that many of our results in this unit are stated for a punctured disc only, but in fact are true for the punctured plane as well. We do not usually point this out explicitly.

It might be supposed that in order to show that a singularity is removable, we proceed by actually calculating the derivative of the function

$$z \longrightarrow \begin{cases} f(z), & z \neq \alpha \\ a, & z = \alpha \end{cases}$$

at the point α. In fact it is almost invariably the case that we use the same sort of technique that we used to show that the singularity of $z \longrightarrow (\sin z)/z$ at 0 is removable, namely: find an alternative representation of the function which is known to be analytic on a disc centre α; in other words, find a function g analytic on a disc centre α such that $g(z) = f(z)$ for $z \neq \alpha$.

We have made our classification of singularities exhaustive by simply bundling together all singularities which are not removable and are not poles and calling them essential. This may seem an arbitrary procedure, but it will become clear that it is a sensible one.

Self-Assessment Question 1

Write down *all* the points at which the following functions have singularities.

(i) $f(z) = z \sin \dfrac{1}{z}$.

(ii) $f(z) = \dfrac{z + 1}{(z - 1)(z^2 + 2iz - 1)}$.

(iii) $f(z) = \dfrac{z - i}{z^2 + 1}$.

(iv) $f(z) = \operatorname{cosec} z$.

(v) $f(z) = \begin{cases} z, & z \neq 0 \\ 1, & z = 0. \end{cases}$

Solution

(i)   0.

(ii)   1, $-i$. (Note that $z^2 + 2iz - 1 = (z + i)^2$.)

(iii) $i, -i$. (The function given is not defined at i, which is therefore a singularity. The fact that the numerator and denominator have the common factor $(z - i)$ means, as you will see later, that the singularity is removable.)

(iv) $\{n\pi : n = 0, \pm 1, \pm 2, \ldots\}$. (These are just the points at which sin is zero.)

(v)   0.

What Kind of Singularity?

The aim of the rest of this section is to develop some methods for identifying the type of a given singularity—in other words whether it is removable, a pole, or essential. We begin with removable singularities.

The simplest way of constructing a function with a removable singularity is to use our first example, $z \longrightarrow (\sin z)/z$, as a model. Let ϕ be a function analytic on a disc $|z - \alpha| < r$, and let

$$f(z) = \frac{\phi(z) - \phi(\alpha)}{z - \alpha}, \text{ when } 0 < |z - \alpha| < r.$$

The function f certainly has a singularity at α (it is not defined there); and if we note that $z \longrightarrow (\sin z)/z$ is a particular case of this construction, we may guess, correctly, that α is a removable singularity.

Lemma

If ϕ is analytic on the disc $|z - \alpha| < r$, and $f(z) = \dfrac{\phi(z) - \phi(\alpha)}{z - \alpha}$ when $0 < |z - \alpha| < r$, then α is a removable singularity of f, which may be removed by setting $f(\alpha) = \phi'(\alpha)$.

Proof

By Theorem 10 of *Unit 6*, there is a function g analytic on the disc $|z - \alpha| < r$ such that

$$\phi(z) = \phi(\alpha) + (z - \alpha) g(z),$$

and $g(\alpha) = \phi'(\alpha)$. But then

$$g(z) = \frac{\phi(z) - \phi(\alpha)}{z - \alpha} = f(z) \qquad \text{for } 0 < |z - \alpha| < r.$$

We conclude that the function

$$z \longrightarrow \begin{cases} f(z), & z \neq \alpha, \\ \phi'(\alpha), & z = \alpha \end{cases}$$

is analytic on the disc $|z - \alpha| < r$, and so α is a removable singularity of f and is removed by setting $f(\alpha) = \phi'(\alpha)$. ∎

This lemma is quite useful in its own right, but its main value is in proving the following theorem, which is the standard test for finding whether or not a singularity is removable.

Theorem 1

If f has a singularity at α and $\lim\limits_{z \to \alpha} (z - \alpha) f(z) = 0$, then α is a removable singularity of f.

11

It is not too difficult to see what $f(\alpha)$ should be in order to remove the singularity. Since Cauchy's Formula must hold when the singularity has been removed, if C is a circle centre α contained in the punctured disc $0 < |z - \alpha| < r$ on which f is analytic, we should have $f(\alpha) = \dfrac{1}{2\pi i} \displaystyle\int_C \dfrac{f(\zeta)}{\zeta - \alpha} \, d\zeta$. More generally, we should *expect* that if z lies inside C, then $f(z) = \dfrac{1}{2\pi i} \displaystyle\int_C \dfrac{f(\zeta)}{\zeta - z} \, d\zeta$. This suggests that we consider the function $z \longrightarrow \dfrac{1}{2\pi i} \displaystyle\int_C \dfrac{f(\zeta)}{\zeta - z} \, d\zeta$, for z inside C (that is, for $|z - \alpha| < \rho$ where ρ is the radius of C, $0 < \rho < r$). This function is analytic on the disc $|z - \alpha| < \rho$, as follows from Problem 6 in Section 5.6 of *Unit 5, Cauchy's Theorem I*. We shall have proved the theorem *if we can establish* that

$$f(z) = \frac{1}{2\pi i} \int_C \frac{f(\zeta)}{\zeta - z} \, d\zeta \qquad \text{for } 0 < |z - \alpha| < \rho.$$

We cannot apply Cauchy's Formula directly because of the singularity of f at α: we do not know that f satisfies the necessary hypotheses. However, we shall be able to show that if $\tilde{C}$ is another circle centre α, and z does *not* lie inside $\tilde{C}$ (Fig. 1), then

$$f(z) = \frac{1}{2\pi i} \int_C \frac{f(\zeta)}{\zeta - z} \, d\zeta - \frac{1}{2\pi i} \int_{\tilde{C}} \frac{f(\zeta)}{\zeta - z} \, d\zeta.$$

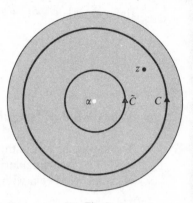

Fig. 1

When we have established this result, we can estimate the second integral, and show that it must be 0, by using the hypothesis that $\lim\limits_{z \to \alpha} (z - \alpha) f(z) = 0$ and by taking the radius of $\tilde{C}$ to be sufficiently small. We can now give details.

Proof of Theorem 1

Our first task is to show that

$$f(z) = \frac{1}{2\pi i} \int_C \frac{f(\zeta)}{\zeta - z} \, d\zeta - \frac{1}{2\pi i} \int_{\tilde{C}} \frac{f(\zeta)}{\zeta - z} \, d\zeta,$$

but it is easier if we reorganize the statement slightly.

Since z lies inside C, $\dfrac{1}{2\pi i} \displaystyle\int_C \dfrac{1}{\zeta - z} \, d\zeta = 1$, by Cauchy's Formula, and so $f(z) = \dfrac{1}{2\pi i} \displaystyle\int_C \dfrac{f(z)}{\zeta - z} \, d\zeta$. But z lies outside $\tilde{C}$, so $\displaystyle\int_{\tilde{C}} \dfrac{1}{\zeta - z} \, d\zeta = 0$, by Cauchy's Theorem. Thus our task is equally to prove that

$$\frac{1}{2\pi i} \int_C \frac{f(z)}{\zeta - z} \, d\zeta = \frac{1}{2\pi i} \int_C \frac{f(\zeta)}{\zeta - z} \, d\zeta - \frac{1}{2\pi i} \int_{\tilde{C}} \frac{f(\zeta)}{\zeta - z} \, d\zeta + \frac{f(z)}{2\pi i} \int_{\tilde{C}} \frac{1}{\zeta - z} \, d\zeta,$$

that is, on rearranging,

$$\frac{1}{2\pi i} \int_C \frac{f(\zeta) - f(z)}{\zeta - z} \, d\zeta = \frac{1}{2\pi i} \int_{\tilde{C}} \frac{f(\zeta) - f(z)}{\zeta - z} \, d\zeta.$$

Consider then the function $\zeta \longrightarrow \dfrac{f(\zeta) - f(z)}{\zeta - z}$, where $0 < |\zeta - \alpha| < r$ and $\zeta \neq z$. This function is analytic on the region $\{\zeta : 0 < |\zeta - \alpha| < r \text{ and } \zeta \neq z\}$. It has a singularity at z (since there is certainly a punctured disc with centre z, on which the function is analytic); but it is a removable singularity, by the lemma; in fact, the function

$$F(\zeta) = \begin{cases} \dfrac{f(\zeta) - f(z)}{\zeta - z}, & \zeta \neq z \\[2mm] f'(z), & \zeta = z \end{cases}$$

is analytic on the punctured disc $0 < |\zeta - \alpha| < r$. (The singularity of F at α does not concern us.) We can therefore apply the deformation lemma of Section 5.5 of *Unit 5* (page 75) to deduce that

$$\frac{1}{2\pi i}\int_C F(\zeta)d\zeta = \frac{1}{2\pi i}\int_{\tilde{C}} F(\zeta)\,d\zeta,$$

which is what we wanted to prove.

We now estimate $\dfrac{1}{2\pi i}\displaystyle\int_{\tilde{C}}\frac{f(\zeta)}{\zeta - z}\,d\zeta$. Let $\varepsilon > 0$, and let $\delta > 0$ be such that

$$|\zeta - \alpha| \cdot |f(\zeta)| < \varepsilon \text{ whenever } |\zeta - \alpha| < \delta.$$

If we require that $\tilde{\rho}$, the radius of $\tilde{C}$, be less than δ, then $\tilde{\rho}\cdot|f(\zeta)| < \varepsilon$ for ζ on $\tilde{C}$. We also have to deal with $1/(\zeta - z)$. Now $|\zeta - z| \geqslant |z - \alpha| - \tilde{\rho} > 0$ when ζ lies on $\tilde{C}$ (Fig. 2). So if we also require that $\tilde{\rho} < \frac{1}{2}|z - \alpha|$, then $|\zeta - z| \geqslant \frac{1}{2}|z - \alpha|$. Thus

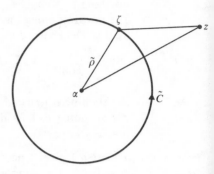

Fig. 2

$$\left|\frac{1}{2\pi i}\int_{\tilde{C}}\frac{f(\zeta)}{\zeta - z}\,d\zeta\right| \leqslant \frac{1}{2\pi}\int_{\tilde{C}}\left|\frac{f(\zeta)}{\zeta - z}\right|\cdot|d\zeta|$$

$$\leqslant \frac{1}{2\pi}\cdot\frac{\varepsilon}{\tilde{\rho}}\cdot\frac{2}{|z - \alpha|}\cdot 2\pi\tilde{\rho}, \quad \text{by the Estimation Theorem,}$$

$$= \frac{2\varepsilon}{|z - \alpha|}.$$

To sum up: if $\tilde{\rho} < \min(\delta, \frac{1}{2}|z - \alpha|)$, then

$$\left|\frac{1}{2\pi i}\int_C\frac{f(\zeta)}{\zeta - z}\,d\zeta\right| \leqslant \frac{2\varepsilon}{|z - \alpha|}.$$

This means that

$$\left|f(z) - \frac{1}{2\pi i}\int_C\frac{f(\zeta)}{\zeta - z}\,d\zeta\right| \leqslant \frac{2\varepsilon}{|z - \alpha|},$$

and since this inequality must hold for every positive ε, we conclude that

$$f(z) = \frac{1}{2\pi i}\int_C\frac{f(\zeta)}{\zeta - z}\,d\zeta \quad \text{for } 0 < |z - \alpha| < r.$$

But since the integral defines a function analytic on the whole disc $|z - \alpha| < r$, we see that f has a removable singularity at α. ∎

Corollary

If f has a singularity at α and $\lim\limits_{z \to \alpha} f(z)$ exists, then f has a removable singularity at α, which is removed by setting $f(\alpha) = \lim\limits_{z \to \alpha} f(z)$.

Proof

If $\lim\limits_{z \to \alpha} f(z)$ exists then $\lim\limits_{z \to \alpha}(z - \alpha)f(z) = 0$, so Theorem 1 applies. We certainly require that f becomes continuous at α when the singularity is removed, which necessitates defining $f(\alpha) = \lim\limits_{z \to \alpha} f(z)$. ∎

Note that during the proof of Theorem 1 we established the following theorem, without restriction on the type of singularity of f at α.

Theorem 2 (Cauchy's Formula for a Punctured Disc)

Suppose that f is analytic on the punctured disc $0 < |z - \alpha| < r$ and that C_1 and C_2 are circles centre α, radii ρ_1 and ρ_2 respectively, where $0 < \rho_1 < \rho_2 < r$. Then

$$f(z) = \frac{1}{2\pi i}\int_{C_2}\frac{f(\zeta)}{\zeta - z}\,d\zeta - \frac{1}{2\pi i}\int_{C_1}\frac{f(\zeta)}{\zeta - z}\,d\zeta,$$

for any z such that $\rho_1 < |z - \alpha| < \rho_2$.

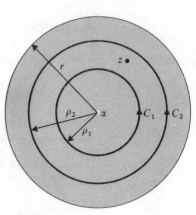

Fig. 3

We call this theorem Cauchy's Formula for a punctured disc because it can be interpreted as representing $f(z)$ as an integral along a contour enclosing z, and is thus a generalization of Cauchy's Formula. An appropriate contour, Γ, is obtained by joining C_1 and C_2 (Fig. 3) by a straight line as shown in Fig. 4. The integrals along the line segment cancel, and C_1 is traversed in the negative (that is, clockwise) direction, so

$$f(z) = \frac{1}{2\pi i} \int_\Gamma \frac{f(\zeta)}{\zeta - z} \, d\zeta.$$

We shall need to use this theorem again later in the unit: this perhaps justifies our spending so long discussing removable singularities, which are otherwise not very important.

Theorem 1 gives a necessary, as well as a sufficient condition, for a removable singularity. For suppose α is a removable singularity of f, and suppose that setting $f(\alpha) = a$ removes the singularity. Then the function

$$z \longrightarrow \begin{cases} f(z), & z \neq \alpha \\ a, & z = \alpha \end{cases}$$

is analytic on the open disc $|z - \alpha| < r$, and so in particular it is continuous at α.

Thus, $\lim\limits_{z \to \alpha} (z - \alpha) f(z) = \left(\lim\limits_{z \to \alpha} (z - \alpha) \right) \cdot a = 0.$

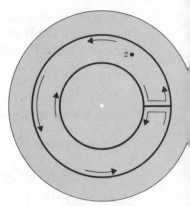

The contour Γ

Fig. 4

Examples

1. That the function $z \longrightarrow (\sin z)/z$ has a removable singularity at 0 is clear. But

    $$\lim_{z \to 0} z \cdot \frac{\cos z}{z} = \lim_{z \to 0} \cos z = 1,$$

    so the singularity of $z \longrightarrow (\cos z)/z$ at 0 is not removable.

2. The function $z \longrightarrow (\sin^2 z)/z^2$ has a removable singularity at 0, since

    $$\lim_{z \to 0} z \cdot \frac{\sin^2 z}{z^2} = \lim_{z \to 0} \sin z \cdot \frac{\sin z}{z} = 0.$$

3. The function $z \longrightarrow z/\sin z$ has a removable singularity at 0, since

    $$\lim_{z \to 0} z \cdot \frac{z}{\sin z} = \left(\lim_{z \to 0} z \right) \cdot \left(\lim_{z \to 0} \frac{z}{\sin z} \right) = 0.$$

4. *Rational Functions.* If p and q are polynomials, then the zeros of q are singularities of the function p/q. If $q(\alpha) = 0$ but $p(\alpha) \neq 0$, then α cannot be a removable singularity of p/q. To see that this is so, note that if $q(\alpha) = 0$ we can write $q(z) = (z - \alpha) \cdot r(z)$, where r is a polynomial (see Problem 6, Section 1.2 of *Unit 1, Complex Numbers*); so

    $$(z - \alpha) \frac{p(z)}{q(z)} = \frac{p(z)}{r(z)},$$

    and this can have limit 0 as z approaches α only if $p(\alpha) = 0$. Thus, for example, $z \longrightarrow (z + i)/(z^2 + 1)$ has a singularity at i which is not removable. It also has a singularity at $-i$, and this one is removable:

    $$\lim_{z \to -i} (z + i) \cdot \frac{z + i}{z^2 + 1} = \lim_{z \to -i} \frac{z + i}{z - i} = 0.$$

    The moral should be clear: if you can factorize p and q then it is easy to see which singularities of p/q are removable.

    It is not always obvious how to factorize polynomials however. Consider the function

    $$z \longrightarrow \frac{z^4 + iz^3 + 7z^2 - 7iz - 2}{(z - i)[z^4 + (1 - i)z^3 - iz^2 + z - i]}.$$

14

It evidently has a singularity at i, and the value of the numerator at i is 0, so it may well be removable. To decide, we have to calculate $\lim\limits_{z \to i} \dfrac{z^4 + iz^3 + 7z^2 - 7iz - 2}{z^4 + (1 - i)z^3 - iz^2 + z - i}$. The denominator is 0 at i also, so we cannot immediately tell what the limit is; and to take out the factors $(z - i)$ from numerator and denominator looks an unpleasant task. But this is just the sort of situation for which l'Hôpital's Rule is designed. (L'Hôpital's Rule is discussed in Problem 2, Section 6.8 of *Unit 6*.) If we apply it, we get

$$\lim_{z \to i} \frac{z^4 + iz^3 + 7z^2 - 7iz - 2}{z^4 + (1 - i)z^3 - iz^2 + z - i} = \lim_{z \to i} \frac{4z^3 + 3iz^2 + 14z - 7i}{4z^3 + 3(1 - i)z^2 - 2iz + 1} = 0$$

since the numerator is 0 at i, but the denominator is not. We conclude that the function has a removable singularity at i.

We turn now to the consideration of poles. Suppose that we have found a singularity of some function, and decided that it is not removable. We want to know if it is a pole, and, if so, what its order is.

Remember that α is a pole of f, of order m, if we can write $f(z) = g(z)/(z - \alpha)^m$ for $z \neq \alpha$, where g is analytic on the disc $|z - \alpha| < r$, and $g(\alpha) \neq 0$. So the first thing to check is whether the function in question is already in the required form. If it is, we can immediately recognize the singularity as a pole and read off its order. For example, $z \longrightarrow (\cos z)/z$ has a pole of order 1 (a simple pole) at 0, since $\cos 0 \neq 0$. It is even easier to see that $z \longrightarrow 1/(z - 3i)^2$ has a pole of order 2 at $3i$.

However it is not necessarily the case that the function will be in the required form, and so we need a more general test. Notice that if f has a pole of order m at α then $\lim\limits_{z \to \alpha} (z - \alpha)^m f(z)$ exists and is non-zero. It turns out that this is a sufficient, as well as a necessary, condition for a pole of order m.

Theorem 3

If f has a singularity at α and $\lim\limits_{z \to \alpha} (z - \alpha)^m f(z)$ exists and is non-zero, then α is a pole of f of order m.

Proof

The function $z \longrightarrow (z - \alpha)^m f(z)$ possibly has a singularity at α, but since $\lim\limits_{z \to \alpha} (z - \alpha)^m f(z)$ exists, the singularity is removable, by the corollary to Theorem 1. Thus if

$$g(z) = \begin{cases} (z - \alpha)^m f(z), & z \neq \alpha \\[2mm] \lim\limits_{z \to \alpha} (z - \alpha)^m f(z), & z = \alpha, \end{cases}$$

then g is analytic on the disc $|z - \alpha| < r$, $g(\alpha) \neq 0$, and $f(z) = g(z)/(z - \alpha)^m$ for $0 < |z - \alpha| < r$.

We conclude that α is a pole of f of order m. ∎

This theorem has a useful corollary, which shows that there is a simple relationship between poles and zeros.

Corollary

Suppose that the function ϕ is analytic on a disc with centre α and has a zero of order m at α. Then $1/\phi$ has a pole of order m at α.

Proof

Since the zeros of a non-zero analytic function are isolated, there is a neighbourhood of α which contains no zeros of ϕ other than α itself. (See Corollary 1 to Theorem 15 of *Unit 6*.) Thus $1/\phi$ is analytic on a punctured neighbourhood of α and is not defined at α and so α is a singularity of $1/\phi$. Moreover, by Theorem 14 of *Unit 6*.

$$\phi(z) = (z - \alpha)^m g(z)$$

where g is analytic on a neighbourhood of α and $g(\alpha) \neq 0$. Thus

$$\lim_{z \to \alpha} \frac{(z - \alpha)^m}{\phi(z)} = \lim_{z \to \alpha} \frac{1}{g(z)} = \frac{1}{g(\alpha)} \neq 0.$$

It follows from Theorem 3 that $1/\phi$ has a pole of order m at α. ∎

Examples

5. The function $z \longrightarrow (z + i)/(z^2 + 1)$ has a singularity at i which is not removable. Since $\dfrac{z + i}{z^2 + 1} = \dfrac{1}{z - i}$ in a punctured disc centre i, the singularity is a simple pole.

6. The function $z \longrightarrow \dfrac{\sin z}{z^m}$, where m is an integer and $m \geqslant 2$, has a singularity at 0 which is not removable. Now

$$\lim_{z \to 0} z^{m-1} \cdot \frac{\sin z}{z^m} = \lim_{z \to 0} \frac{\sin z}{z} = 1,$$

so the singularity is a pole of order $m - 1$.

7. By considering the Taylor series of the function $z \longrightarrow \sin(z^2)$, it is clear that it has a zero of order 2 at 0, so $z \longrightarrow 1/\sin(z^2)$ has a pole of order 2 at 0.

Summary

In this section we explained the term "singularity of a function" and gave a classification of singularities into three types—removable singularities, poles, and essential singularities—together with methods for recognizing the type of a given singularity. It is important that you remember these definitions and methods because we shall be using them repeatedly in this unit and later in the course.

Self-Assessment Questions

2. The function $z \longrightarrow \tan 1/z$ is defined on **C** except at the points $1/(n\pi + \pi/2)$, $n = \pm 1, \pm 2, \ldots$, and at 0. Where are its singularities? (Note: $\tan = \sin/\cos$.)

3. Fill in the blanks using the following options. Options: a removable singularity, a pole, an essential singularity.

   (i) If f has a singularity at α and there is a function g analytic on the disc $|z - \alpha| < r$, with $g(\alpha) \neq 0$, such that $f(z) = g(z)/(z - \alpha)^m$ for $z \neq \alpha$, where m is a positive integer, then f has

   ⬚ at α.

   (ii) If f has a singularity at α and there is a function g analytic on the disc $|z - \alpha| < r$ such that $f(z) = g(z)$, for $z \neq \alpha$, then f has

   ⬚ at α.

4. Suppose that the function f has a singularity at 0. For each of the following cases, state what kind of singularity it is if the given statement is true.

(i) $f(z) = \dfrac{\phi(z)}{z}$, $z \neq 0$, where ϕ is entire and $\phi(0) = 0$.

(ii) $f(z) = \dfrac{\phi(z)}{z}$, $z \neq 0$, where ϕ is entire and $\phi(0) \neq 0$.

(iii) $\lim\limits_{z \to 0} z^m f(z)$ does not exist for any positive integer m.

(iv) $\lim\limits_{z \to 0} z^m f(z) = 0$, where m is an integer and $m \geqslant 2$.
   (Hint: What can you say about the function $z \longrightarrow z^{m-1} f(z)$?)

(v) $f(z) = \dfrac{1}{\phi(z)}$, $z \neq 0$, where ϕ is entire and has just one zero, a zero of order 1 at 0.

Solutions

2. The function $z \longrightarrow \tan 1/z$ has singularities at the points $1/(n\pi + \pi/2)$, $n = \pm 1, \pm 2, \ldots$. Although the function is not defined at 0, this point is not an isolated point of the set $\{0\} \cup \left\{ \dfrac{1}{n\pi + \pi/2} : n = \pm 1, \pm 2, \ldots \right\}$, and so cannot be a singularity.

3. (i) a pole. (ii) a removable singularity.

4. (i) Removable singularity.

(ii) Simple pole.

(iii) Essential singularity. (The singularity cannot be removable, since $\lim\limits_{z \to 0} z f(z)$ does not exist, and cannot be a pole, since $\lim\limits_{z \to 0} z^m f(z)$ does not exist for $m \geqslant 1$.)

(iv) Pole of order at most $m - 1$, or removable singularity. (Since $\lim\limits_{z \to 0} z \cdot z^{m-1} f(z) = 0$, the function $z \longrightarrow z^{m-1} f(z)$ has a removable singularity at 0. Thus $\lim\limits_{z \to 0} z^{m-1} f(z)$ exists; if it is non-zero, f has a pole of order $m - 1$ at 0; if it is zero, begin again.)

(v) Simple pole.

8.2 PROBLEMS

1. Find all the singularities of the following functions, and classify them as removable singularities, poles, or essential singularities. Give the order of any poles.

   (i) $z \longrightarrow \dfrac{\cos z}{z^2}$.

   (ii) $z \longrightarrow \dfrac{1}{(1 - z)(2 - z)}$.

   (iii) $z \longrightarrow \dfrac{z^5 - 2z^4 + z - 2}{z - 2}$.

   (iv) $z \longrightarrow \dfrac{z^3 + (1 - i)z^2 + (1 - i)z - i}{z^2 - (1 + i)z + i}$.

   (v) $z \longrightarrow \tan z$.

   (vi) $z \longrightarrow \dfrac{1}{e^z}$.

   (vii) $z \longrightarrow \exp(z + 1/z)$.

   (viii) $z \longrightarrow \dfrac{z}{e^z - 1}$.

   (ix) $z \longrightarrow \dfrac{1}{z^2(z^2 + 1)}$.

   (x) $z \longrightarrow p(1/z)$, where p is a polynomial of degree m.

2. (i) Show that if f is analytic on the punctured disc $0 < |z - \alpha| < r$, and is bounded on the disc $|z - \alpha| < r$, then f has a removable singularity at α.

   (ii) Show that a function which is continuous on an open disc $|z - \alpha| < r$, and analytic on the punctured disc $0 < |z - \alpha| < r$, is necessarily differentiable at α.

3. Suppose that the function f has a pole of order m at α, and the function g has a pole of order n at α, where $m > n$. What type of singularity at α do the functions (i) $f + g$ and (ii) $f \cdot g$ have? What difference does it make if $n = m$?

4. Show that the singularities of a rational function are either removable, or are poles.

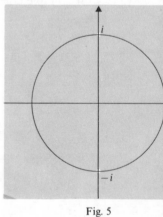

Fig. 5

The Taylor series for the function $z \longrightarrow 1/(1 + z^2)$ about 0 has radius of convergence 1, as we pointed out in *Unit 6*. The function has non-removable singularities (that is, singularities which are not removable) at i and $-i$ (simple poles, in fact). These singularities are both distance 1 from 0; in other words, they lie on the circle of convergence of the Taylor series. It looks as though it is the presence of the singularities which limits the set on which the Taylor series converges. The next problem is concerned with this hypothesis.

5. Suppose that the function f has a finite number of singularities $\alpha_1, \alpha_2, \ldots, \alpha_n$ but is analytic on $\mathbf{C} - \{\alpha_1, \alpha_2, \ldots, \alpha_n\}$. Let β be a point of $\mathbf{C} - \{\alpha_1, \alpha_2, \ldots, \alpha_n\}$. Show that the radius of convergence of the Taylor series for f about β is the distance from β to the nearest non-removable singularity of f (or nearest non-removable singularities, if there are several). (You may find the following result, Corollary 1 to Theorem 16 of *Unit 6*, helpful: If f and g are analytic on a region R, and if $f = g$ on a nonempty open set in R, then $f = g$ on R.)

Solutions

1. (i) Pole of order 2 at 0.

   (ii) Simple poles at 1 and 2.

   (iii) Removable singularity at 2.

   (iv) Removable singularity at i; simple pole at 1.

   (v) Simple poles at $\dfrac{\pi}{2} + n\pi$, $n = 0, \pm 1, \pm 2, \dots$.

   (vi) No singularities.

   (vii) Essential singularity at 0.

   (viii) Removable singularity at 0; simple poles at $2ni\pi$, $n = \pm 1, \pm 2, \dots$.

   (ix) Pole of order 2 at 0; simple poles at $\pm i$.

   (x) Pole of order m at 0.

2. (i) Suppose that $|f(z)| \leqslant K$ on the disc $|z - \alpha| < r$. Then $|(z - \alpha)f(z)| \leqslant |z - \alpha| \cdot K$, and so $\lim\limits_{z \to \alpha} (z - \alpha)f(z) = 0$. Thus f has a removable singularity at α, by Theorem 1.

   (ii) If f is continuous on the disc $|z - \alpha| < r$, then $\lim\limits_{z \to \alpha} f(z)$ exists, so by the corollary to Theorem 1, f has a removable singularity at α, which is removed by setting $f(\alpha) = \lim\limits_{z \to \alpha} f(z)$. But the continuity of f means that the singularity has already been removed, that is, that f is analytic on the whole disc, and in particular that f is differentiable at α.

3. (i) The function $f + g$ has a pole of order m at α.

   Since $m > n$, we have
   $$\lim_{z \to \alpha} (z - \alpha)^m (f(z) + g(z)) = \lim_{z \to \alpha} (z - \alpha)^m f(z)$$
   $$+ \lim_{z \to \alpha} (z - \alpha)^{m-n} \lim_{z \to \alpha} (z - \alpha)^n g(z)$$
   $$= \lim_{z \to \alpha} (z - \alpha)^m f(z) \neq 0.$$

   Thus by Theorem 3, $f + g$ has a pole of order m at α.

   (ii) The function $f \cdot g$ has a pole of order $m + n$ at α.

   In fact
   $$\lim_{z \to \alpha} (z - \alpha)^{m+n} f(z) \cdot g(z) = \lim_{z \to \alpha} (z - \alpha)^m f(z) \cdot \lim_{z \to \alpha} (z - \alpha)^n g(z)$$
   $$\neq 0.$$
   Thus $f \cdot g$ has a pole of order $m + n$ at α.

   If $m = n$, so that f and g both have poles of order m at α, then $f \cdot g$ has a pole of order $2m$ at α, but $f + g$ need not have a pole of order m at α. Indeed $f + g$ need not have a pole at all: $g = -f$, for example. The most that can be said is that $f + g$ has a pole whose order does not exceed m, or it has a removable singularity.

4. The singularities of a rational function occur at the zeros of its denominator. Suppose $f(z) = p(z)/q(z)$, and $q(\alpha) = 0$. Then we can write $q(z) = (z - \alpha)^n \tilde{q}(z)$, where $\tilde{q}(\alpha) \neq 0$. It is possible that $p(\alpha) = 0$ also. Then we can write $p(z) = (z - \alpha)^m \tilde{p}(z)$, where $\tilde{p}(\alpha) \neq 0$. If $m \geqslant n$, the singularity is removable, since $\lim\limits_{z \to \alpha} (z - \alpha)f(z) = 0$; whereas if $m < n$, the singularity is a pole of order $n - m$, since
   $$\lim_{z \to \alpha} (z - \alpha)^{n-m} f(z) = \frac{\tilde{p}(\alpha)}{q(\alpha)} \neq 0.$$

5. Suppose that α is the *non-removable* singularity of f nearest β (or any one of the nearest non-removable singularities, if there are several). Then f is analytic on the disc $|z - \beta| < |\alpha - \beta|$, and so its Taylor series about α certainly converges on that disc. In other words, if ρ is the radius of convergence of the Taylor series for f about α, then $\rho \geqslant |\alpha - \beta|$. We wish to show that $\rho = |\alpha - \beta|$. We may argue by contradiction.

Suppose that $\rho > |\alpha - \beta|$. Then the Taylor series would define a function g, which would be analytic on the disc $|z - \beta| < \rho$, and satisfy $g(z) = f(z)$ when $|z - \beta| < |\alpha - \beta|$. Now f is analytic on the region R obtained by removing from the disc $|z - \beta| < \rho$ those points, finite in number, at which f has a singularity. Since g would also be analytic on R, and would agree with f on a nonempty open subset of R (namely the open disc $|z - \beta| < |\alpha - \beta|$), it would follow that $g = f$ on R (by Corollary 1 to Theorem 16 of *Unit 6*). But g would be analytic on the whole of the disc $|z - \beta| < \rho$, and this would mean that all the singularities of f in this disc, including the one at α, were removable, contradicting the assumption that α is a *non-removable* singularity nearest β.

We conclude that $\rho = |\alpha - \beta|$.

8.3 ESSENTIAL SINGULARITIES

An essential singularity is a singularity which is not removable and not a pole. One might imagine that there is not very much of interest that can be said about essential singularities. The nature of the definition suggests this: we have simply thrown all the singularities we do not like the look of into a dustbin and labelled it "essential."

In fact, essential singularities are very interesting.

In the first place, an essential singularity, is very palpably singular, in comparison with a removable singularity or a pole. A removable singularity is a singularity only by accident anyway, and a pole is such a simple kind of singularity that one can learn to live with it. An essential singularity, on the other hand, cannot be ignored. It is in this sense that it is essential.

Secondly, and less fancifully, functions with essential singularities have interesting and surprising properties. It is with one of these properties that we shall be concerned in this short section.

In fact, we shall be concerned with comparing the behaviour of a function near a pole and a function near an essential singularity. The examples of Section 8.1 are useful once again: they typify the sort of thing we have in mind. You will remember that $z \longrightarrow (\cos z)/z$ has a simple pole at 0, whereas $z \longrightarrow \exp 1/z$ has an essential singularity there. In Section 8.1 we showed that neither has a limit near 0. We wish to examine the way in which each function fails to have a limit near 0.

The function $z \longrightarrow (\cos z)/z$ does not have a limit near 0 simply because its modulus gets bigger and bigger as z gets closer and closer to 0. A natural way of expressing this is to say that

$$\lim_{z \to 0} \frac{\cos z}{z} = \infty;$$

and if we define the symbols correctly this expression describes the behaviour of $z \longrightarrow (\cos z)/z$ precisely.

Definition

> $\lim\limits_{z \to \alpha} f(z) = \infty$ means that given any positive number N, there is a positive number δ such that
>
> $$|f(z)| > N \text{ whenever } 0 < |z - \alpha| < \delta.$$

If you look back at Section 8.1 you will see that we proved there that $\lim\limits_{z \to 0} \dfrac{\cos z}{z} = \infty$ according to this definition.

Now $z \longrightarrow \exp 1/z$ behaves quite differently as z approaches 0. It is true that if z is small, real and positive, then $|\exp 1/z|$ is large; but if z is small, real and negative then $|\exp 1/z|$ is small. In fact the function jigs about all over the place. It is easy to show that if δ is any given positive number, and w is any non-zero complex number, then there is a complex number z such that $\exp 1/z = w$, and $0 < |z| < \delta$. In other words, the function takes on *all* non-zero complex values in *every* punctured disc around 0, however small. That, you must admit, is a remarkable fact. Its proof is quite simple. Let L be a branch of the logarithm which contains w in its domain. Then the solutions of the equation $\exp 1/z = w$ are the complex numbers

$$z = \frac{1}{L(w) + 2ni\pi}, \quad n = 0, \pm 1, \pm 2, \ldots.$$

21

By choosing a large enough n, we may take z as small as we please. To be precise, if $n > \dfrac{1}{2\pi}\left(\dfrac{1}{\delta} + |L(w)|\right)$ then $\left|\dfrac{1}{L(w) + 2ni\pi}\right| < \delta$, because

$$|L(w) + 2ni\pi| \geqslant \|2ni\pi| - |L(w)\|$$

$$= 2n\pi - |L(w)| > \frac{1}{\delta}.$$

These two examples are typical. That $z \longrightarrow (\cos z)/z$ typifies behaviour near a pole is reflected in a theorem we shall prove presently, which says that $\lim\limits_{z \to \alpha} f(z) = \infty$ is a necessary and sufficient condition for α to be a pole of f. So far as essential singularities are concerned, it is true that if α is an essential singularity of f, then f assumes all complex values with possibly one exception on any punctured disc centre α. (Note that $\exp 1/z$ can *never* be 0; hence the qualification "with possibly one exception".) It is true, but it is difficult to prove. We must be content with a somewhat weaker, but still remarkable, result, which is known as the Casorati–Weierstrass Theorem.*

The remainder of this section is devoted to the proofs of these two theorems.

Theorem 4

Suppose that f has a singularity at α. The condition $\lim\limits_{z \to \alpha} f(z) = \infty$ is a necessary and sufficient condition for α to be a pole of f.

Proof

(i) Necessity.   If α is a pole of f, then $f(z) = \dfrac{g(z)}{(z - \alpha)^m}, z \neq \alpha$, for some analytic function g and positive integer m where $g(\alpha) \neq 0$. But $\lim\limits_{z \to \alpha} \dfrac{g(z)}{(z - \alpha)^m} = \infty$ (see Problem 2, Section 8.4).

(ii) Sufficiency.   Suppose that $\lim\limits_{z \to \alpha} f(z) = \infty$. Then there is some $r > 0$ such that $f(z)$ is never zero for $0 < |z - \alpha| < r$. Let $F(z) = 1/f(z)$ on the punctured disc $0 < |z - \alpha| < r$. It follows from the condition $\lim\limits_{z \to \alpha} f(z) = \infty$ that $\lim\limits_{z \to \alpha} F(z) = 0$ (again see Problem 2, Section 8.4). If we extend the domain of F to include α by setting $F(\alpha) = 0$, F will be analytic on the disc $|z - \alpha| < r$ by the corollary to Theorem 1. The function F is analytic on the disc $|z - \alpha| < r$ and has an isolated zero at α; thus $F(z) = (z - \alpha)^m h(z)$, where m is the order of the zero, h is analytic on the disc $|z - \alpha| < r$, and $h(\alpha) \neq 0$. Since $h(\alpha) \neq 0$, there is some punctured disc centre α on which h is never zero; on this disc we can define $g(z) = 1/h(z)$; g will be analytic and $g(\alpha)$ will be non-zero. Putting everything together we get

$$f(z) = \frac{1}{F(z)} = \frac{1}{(z - \alpha)^m} \cdot \frac{1}{h(z)} = \frac{g(z)}{(z - \alpha)^m}, \quad z \neq \alpha.$$

Thus α is a pole of f (of order m). ∎

---

* *Felice Casorati* (1835–1890) was professor of mathematics at Pavia, and was one of the founders of the Italian school of analysis. In 1858, he went with two other Italian mathematicians to France and Germany: this journey is often regarded as the beginning of the revival in mathematical interest in Italy. For Weierstrass, see page 43 of *Unit 1*.

Theorem 5 (The Casorati–Weierstrass Theorem)

Suppose that f is analytic on the punctured disc $0 < |z - \alpha| < r$, and that α is an essential singularity of f. Given any complex number w, and any positive real numbers ε and δ, with $\delta < r$, there is a complex number z such that $0 < |z - \alpha| < \delta$ for which $|f(z) - w| < \varepsilon$.

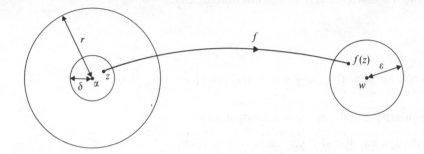

(Before we tackle the proof of this theorem, let us show that it does describe the behaviour of the function $z \longrightarrow \exp 1/z$. If $f(z) = \exp 1/z$, then f is analytic on the punctured plane $0 < |z|$, and has an essential singularity at 0. Let w be any non-zero complex number and ε and δ any positive real numbers: then we can find a complex number z such that $0 < |z| < \delta$ for which $|f(z) - w| < \varepsilon$, since we can in fact find z for which $f(z) - w = 0$. If $w = 0$, on the other hand, and ε and δ are positive real numbers, then we can still find a complex number z such that $0 < |z| < \delta$ for which $|f(z) - w| = |f(z)| < \varepsilon$: we can find z for which $f(z) = \varepsilon/2$, for example. So even though $\exp 1/z$ never takes the value 0, it comes arbitrarily close to it on any punctured disc centre 0.)

Proof

We argue by contradiction. Suppose the assertion were false; that is suppose that there were a complex number w and positive real numbers ε and δ, with $\delta < r$, such that whenever $0 < |z - \alpha| < \delta$ then $|f(z) - w| \geqslant \varepsilon$. (Make sure you understand this negation.) We shall show that α could not be an essential singularity of f.

Since $f(z) - w \neq 0$ on the punctured disc $D = \{z : 0 < |z - \alpha| < \delta\}$, the function $\phi(z) = 1/(f(z) - w)$ would be analytic on D. Moreover, $|\phi(z)| \leqslant 1/\varepsilon$ on D, and so $\lim_{z \to \alpha} (z - \alpha)\phi(z) = 0$. So by Theorem 1, α would be a removable singularity of ϕ, and by defining $\phi(\alpha)$ appropriately we could remove the singularity, and extend ϕ to become analytic on the disc $|z - \alpha| < \delta$.

Now $f(z) = w + 1/\phi(z)$ on D. If $\phi(\alpha) \neq 0$, then f would have a removable singularity at α, which could be removed by setting $f(\alpha) = w + 1/\phi(\alpha)$. If ϕ had a zero of order m at α, so that $\phi(z) = (z - \alpha)^m g(z)$, where $g(\alpha) \neq 0$, then

$$\lim_{z \to \alpha} (z - \alpha)^m f(z) = \lim_{z \to \alpha} (z - \alpha)^m w + \lim_{z \to \alpha} \frac{1}{g(z)} = \frac{1}{g(\alpha)} \neq 0,$$

and f would have a pole of order m at α (by Theorem 3). These would be the only possibilities for ϕ, and in neither case would f have an essential singularity at α.

We conclude that if α is an essential singularity of f then the assertion of the theorem is correct. ∎

Summary

We have been able to analyse the behaviour of a function near a non-removable singularity, and have found that there are dramatic differences between the cases of a pole and an essential singularity. Near a pole the modulus of the function gets large. On the other hand a function approximates every complex value in every disc centred at the singularity, if it is an essential singularity.

Self-Assessment Questions

Fill in the blanks.

1. If f is analytic on the punctured disc $0 < |z - \alpha| < r$ and $\lim\limits_{z \to \alpha} f(z) = \infty$, then α is [   ] .
    Options: a removable singularity, a pole, an essential singularity.

2. If f is analytic on the punctured disc $0 < |z - \alpha| < r$, and $|f(z)| \geqslant 1$ whenever $0 < |z - \alpha| < \frac{1}{2}r$, then α [   ] be an essential singularity of f.

    Options: can, cannot.

Solutions

1. a pole.

2. cannot. By the Casorati–Weierstrass Theorem with $w = 0$, $\varepsilon = 1$, $\delta = \frac{1}{2}r$, if α were an essential singularity there would be some z such that $0 < |z - \alpha| < \frac{1}{2}r$ for which $|f(z)| < 1$.

8.4 PROBLEMS

1.   Show that the Casorati–Weierstrass Theorem may be equivalently stated in either of the following ways:

   (i)   Suppose that f has an essential singularity at α. If w is any complex number, there is a sequence $\{z_n\}$ such that

$$\lim_{n \to \infty} z_n = \alpha \quad \text{and} \quad \lim_{n \to \infty} f(z_n) = w.$$

   (ii) Suppose that f has an essential singularity at α. If D is any punctured disc with centre α, then the closure of the set $\{f(z) : z \in D\}$ is the whole complex plane.

2.   Show that if $f(z) \neq 0$ for $0 < |z - \alpha| < r$, then $\lim\limits_{z \to \alpha} \dfrac{1}{f(z)} = \infty$ if and only if $\lim\limits_{z \to \alpha} f(z) = 0$. More generally, show that if $\lim\limits_{z \to \alpha} g(z)$ exists and is not zero, then $\lim\limits_{z \to \alpha} \dfrac{g(z)}{f(z)} = \infty$ if and only if $\lim\limits_{z \to \alpha} f(z) = 0$.

Solutions

1.   (i)   Suppose that the conclusion of the Casorati–Weierstrass Theorem holds. Then for each positive integer n, there is a complex number z_n such that $|f(z_n) - w| < 1/n$ and $0 < |z_n - \alpha| < 1/n$ (take $\varepsilon = \delta = 1/n$). The sequence $\{z_n\}$ satisfies $\lim\limits_{n \to \infty} z_n = \alpha$ and $\lim\limits_{n \to \infty} f(z_n) = w$. Suppose that a sequence with the given properties exists. Then given any pair of positive numbers ε, δ there is a natural number N_1 such that $0 < |z_n - \alpha| < \delta$ when $n > N_1$, and a natural number N_2 such that $|f(z_n) - w| < \varepsilon$ when $n > N_2$. Then z_N satisfies the conclusion of the Casorati–Weierstrass Theorem if $N \geqslant \max(N_1, N_2)$.

   (ii) Suppose that the conclusion of the Casorati–Weierstrass Theorem holds. Then if $w \in \mathbf{C}$, and ε is a positive number, there is some z in D such that $|f(z) - w| < \varepsilon$. This says that w is a cluster point of the set $\{f(z) : z \in D\}$. Thus the closure of the set is the whole complex plane. Suppose that the closure of $\{f(z) : z \in D\}$ is $\mathbf{C}$ for every punctured disc D centre α. Then if $w \in \mathbf{C}$, and ε and δ are given positive numbers, there is some z in D_δ (the punctured disc centred at α of radius δ) such that $|f(z) - w| < \varepsilon$, because w is a cluster point of $\{f(z) : z \in D_\delta\}$. Thus the conclusion of the Casorati–Weierstrass Theorem holds.

2.   Since $|1/f(z)| > N$ if and only if $|f(z)| < 1/N$, the first part holds.

   For the second part, assume that $\lim\limits_{z \to \alpha} g(z) = \lambda \neq 0$. Then $\frac{3}{2}|\lambda| > |g(z)| > \frac{1}{2}|\lambda|$ on some disc centre α. So if $\left| \dfrac{g(z)}{f(z)} \right| > N$, then $|f(z)| < \frac{3}{2} \cdot \dfrac{|\lambda|}{N}$, whereas if $|f(z)| < \dfrac{1}{N}$, then $\left| \dfrac{g(z)}{f(z)} \right| > \frac{1}{2}|\lambda| \cdot N$.

8.5 LAURENT SERIES ABOUT A POLE

There are still more ideas to be got from the examples of Section 8.1.

The Taylor series for $\cos z$ is

$$1 - \frac{z^2}{2!} + \frac{z^4}{4!} - \cdots ;$$

it converges for every z.

So the series

$$\frac{1}{z} - \frac{z}{2!} + \frac{z^3}{4!} - \cdots$$

converges to $(\cos z)/z$ for every non-zero z; we have a series expansion for our function, and the fact that 0 is a singularity of the function explains, or is explained by, the presence of the term $1/z$ in the series. Such a series (one which involves terms in $1/(z - \alpha)$ as well as terms in $(z - \alpha)$) is called a **Laurent series**; Laurent series play the same role for functions with singularities as Taylor series play for analytic functions. We are about to embark on a study of Laurent series.

We are primarily interested in whether we can find a series expansion like the one we found for $z \longrightarrow (\cos z)/z$, for any function which has a singularity. If the singularity is a pole it is quite easy to prove that such a series expansion is possible, and we shall give the proof shortly. (If the singularity is removable there is no problem—we can use the Taylor series.) But over and above this we are interested in finding some formula for the coefficients of the series. It is very useful to know that the coefficients of the Taylor series are given by the derivatives of the function in question. Is there an analogue for Laurent series? We cannot expect the coefficients to be expressible as derivatives, since the function will not be differentiable at the crucial point. But Cauchy's Formulas allow us to express derivatives as contour integrals. It is as contour integrals, too, that we can express the coefficients in the Laurent series.

Theorem 6

Suppose that f is analytic on the punctured disc $0 < |z - \alpha| < r$ and that α is a pole of order m of f. Let $a_n = \dfrac{1}{2\pi i} \displaystyle\int_C \frac{f(\zeta)}{(\zeta - \alpha)^{n+1}} \, d\zeta$, for $n \geqslant -m$, where C is a circle $|\zeta - \alpha| = \rho$, with $0 < \rho < r$. Then (i) the series $\displaystyle\sum_{n=-m}^{\infty} a_n(z - \alpha)^n$ converges to $f(z)$ for all z such that $0 < |z - \alpha| < r$. Moreover, (ii) this representation of f by a Laurent series is unique: that is, if a series $\displaystyle\sum_{n=-l}^{\infty} b_n(z - \alpha)^n$ also converges to $f(z)$ on the punctured disc $0 < |z - \alpha| < r$, and $b_{-l} \neq 0$, then $l = m$ and $b_n = a_n$ for all $n \geqslant -m$.

Proof

(i) Since α is a pole of order m of f, we may write

$$f(z) = \frac{g(z)}{(z - \alpha)^m} \text{ when } 0 < |z - \alpha| < r,$$

where g is analytic on the disc $|z - \alpha| < r$, and $g(\alpha) \neq 0$. Then

$$a_n = \frac{1}{2\pi i} \int_C \frac{f(\zeta)}{(\zeta - \alpha)^{n+1}} \, d\zeta$$

$$= \frac{1}{2\pi i} \int_C \frac{g(\zeta)}{(\zeta - \alpha)^{m+n+1}} \, d\zeta$$

$$= \frac{g^{(n+m)}(\alpha)}{(n + m)!},$$

using Cauchy's Formulas (Theorems 4, 5 and 8 of *Unit 5*). The series $\sum_{k=0}^{\infty} a_{k-m}(z-\alpha)^k$ is the Taylor series for g, and therefore converges to $g(z)$ for all z such that $|z - \alpha| < r$. Thus if $0 < |z - \alpha| < r$, the series

$$\sum_{k=0}^{\infty} a_{k-m} \frac{(z-\alpha)^k}{(z-\alpha)^m} = \sum_{k=0}^{\infty} a_{k-m}(z-\alpha)^{k-m}$$

$$= \sum_{n=-m}^{\infty} a_n(z-\alpha)^n$$

converges to $\dfrac{g(z)}{(z-\alpha)^m} = f(z)$.

Notice that $a_{-m} = g(\alpha) \neq 0$.

(ii) The uniqueness of the representation has still to be established. We show first that if $\sum_{n=-l}^{\infty} b_n(z-\alpha)^n$, with $b_{-l} \neq 0$, converges to $f(z)$ on the punctured disc $0 < |z - \alpha| < r$, then $l = m$. Now, if $f(z) = \sum_{n=-l}^{\infty} b_n(z-\alpha)^n$, then

$$(z-\alpha)^l f(z) = \sum_{n=-l}^{\infty} b_n(z-\alpha)^{n+l}$$

$$= \sum_{k=0}^{\infty} b_{k-l}(z-\alpha)^k;$$

this power series converges on the disc $|z - \alpha| < r$ to an analytic function whose value at α is b_{-l}. Thus $\lim_{z \to \alpha} (z-\alpha)^l f(z) = b_{-l} \neq 0$, and so by Theorem 3, l is the order of the pole of f at α; that is $l = m$.

Since $\sum_{n=-m}^{\infty} b_n(z-\alpha)^n = f(z) = \sum_{n=-m}^{\infty} a_n(z-\alpha)^n$, for $0 < |z - \alpha| < r$, it follows that

$$\sum_{n=-m}^{\infty} (b_n - a_n)(z-\alpha)^n = 0 \qquad \text{for } 0 < |z - \alpha| < r.$$

So

$$\sum_{k=0}^{\infty} (b_{k-m} - a_{k-m})(z-\alpha)^k = \sum_{n=-m}^{\infty} (b_n - a_n)(z-\alpha)^{n+m}$$

$$= (z-\alpha)^m \sum_{n=-m}^{\infty} (b_n - a_n)(z-\alpha)^n = 0.$$

The power series $\sum_{k=0}^{\infty} (b_{k-m} - a_{k-m})(z-\alpha)^k$ must converge to 0 at α, too, by continuity; it is therefore the Taylor series for the zero function. But this means that all its coefficients vanish. So $b_{k-m} = a_{k-m}$ for $k \geqslant 0$, that is $b_n = a_n$ for $n \geqslant -m$. ∎

Notice that the region of convergence of the Laurent series $\sum_{n=-m}^{\infty} a_n(z-\alpha)^n$ is a punctured disc with centre α. The reason is that the part $\sum_{n=0}^{\infty} a_n(z-\alpha)^n$ is a Taylor series and the function

$$z \longrightarrow \frac{a_{-m}}{(z-\alpha)^m} + \cdots + \frac{a_{-1}}{(z-\alpha)}$$

is analytic everywhere except α. We call the series $\sum_{n=-m}^{\infty} a_n(z-\alpha)^n$ *the Laurent series for f centred at α*, or *the Laurent series for f about α*, convergent on the punctured disc $0 < |z - \alpha| < r$.

It is perhaps worth emphasizing that the highest power of $1/(z - \alpha)$ that occurs in the Laurent series is the order of the pole. Notice, too, that if $n \leqslant -1$ then the *integrand* (that is, the function to be integrated) in the formula for a_n is $f(\zeta)$ multiplied by $(\zeta - \alpha)$ to a *positive* power: so, for example,

$$a_{-2} = \frac{1}{2\pi i} \int_C f(\zeta)(\zeta - \alpha)d\zeta, \quad \text{and} \quad a_{-1} = \frac{1}{2\pi i} \int_C f(\zeta)\, d\zeta.$$

This tends to be obscured by the notation. (Resist the temptation to apply Cauchy's Theorem and conclude that $\int_C f(\zeta)\, d\zeta = 0$; the whole point of the exercise is that the region on which f is analytic and in which C lies is *not* star.) One other point: the reason why we do not have to specify C more exactly is that the deformation lemma of *Unit 5*, Section 5.5, tells us that it does not matter which circle we choose. If C_1 is the circle $|\zeta - \alpha| = \rho_1$ and C_2 is the circle $|\zeta - \alpha| = \rho_2$, where $0 < \rho_1 < r$ and $0 < \rho_2 < r$, then $\int_{C_1} \frac{f(\zeta)}{(\zeta - \alpha)^{n+1}}\, d\zeta = \int_{C_2} \frac{f(\zeta)}{(\zeta - \alpha)^{n+1}}\, d\zeta$, since the integrand is analytic except at α.

The formulas $a_n = \frac{1}{2\pi i} \int_C \frac{f(\zeta)}{(\zeta - \alpha)^{n+1}}\, d\zeta$ are useful for theoretical work, but in practice do not help much in finding the Laurent series for the function f. We cannot adopt the sort of strategy we use for finding Taylor series by differentiation, to find a Laurent series. To calculate the coefficients in a Taylor series we try to find a formula for the nth derivative of the function, usually in the form of a recurrence relation, and often by using Leibniz's formula. We have no convenient tool like Leibniz's formula to enable us to calculate recurrence relations between integrals. To find a Laurent series it is usually necessary to use a method like the one we used to find the series for $z \longrightarrow (\cos z)/z$—a method that involves writing down power series and carrying out various algebraic operations. The uniqueness part of Theorem 6 tells us that a Laurent series obtained in this way is valid. What is more, this gives us a method of finding the orders of poles, and of calculating certain integrals without doing any integration.

Examples

1. Show that the function $z \longrightarrow \dfrac{\sin z}{z^2}$ has a simple pole at 0, by finding its Laurent series centred at 0.

    The Taylor series centred at 0 for sin is

    $$\sin z = z - \frac{z^3}{3!} + \frac{z^5}{5!} - \cdots,$$

    which converges for all z. Thus the series

    $$\frac{1}{z^2}\left(z - \frac{z^3}{3!} + \frac{z^5}{5!} - \cdots\right) = \frac{1}{z} - \frac{z}{3!} + \frac{z^3}{5!} - \cdots$$

    converges to $(\sin z)/z^2$ for $z \neq 0$, and is thus the Laurent series centred at 0 for the function. Since the highest power of $1/z$ which occurs is 1, we conclude that the function has a simple pole at 0.

2. Show that if C is any circle centre 0, then

    $$\int_C \frac{\sin \zeta}{\zeta^2}\, d\zeta = 2\pi i.$$

    By the formula for the coefficient of $1/z$ in the Laurent series in Example 1, we have

    $$a_{-1} = 1 = \frac{1}{2\pi i} \int_C \frac{\sin \zeta}{\zeta^2}\, d\zeta$$

    and the result follows.

3. Find the order of the pole of $z \longrightarrow \dfrac{1}{\sin(z^2)}$ at 0, and calculate $\displaystyle\int_C \dfrac{1}{\sin(\zeta^2)}\, d\zeta$, where C is a circle centre 0.

We have

$$\sin(z^2) = z^2 + z^6\phi(z), \quad \text{where } \phi \text{ is entire,}$$
$$= z^2(1 + z^4\phi(z)),$$

Thus, provided $z \neq 0$,

$$\frac{1}{\sin(z^2)} = \frac{1}{z^2}(1 + z^4\phi(z))^{-1}.$$

Since $\lim\limits_{z \to 0} z^4\phi(z) = 0$, there is a disc centre 0 on which $|z^4\phi(z)| < 1$. On this disc we can expand $(1 + z^4\phi(z))^{-1}$ as a series in powers of $z^4\phi(z)$:

$$(1 + z^4\phi(z))^{-1} = 1 - z^4\phi(z) + (z^4\phi(z))^2 - \cdots.$$

In principle we can expand ϕ in a Taylor series, calculate the powers (as Cauchy products) and sum to give a power series expansion of $(1 + z^4\phi(z))^{-1}$ valid on the disc. We can then multiply by $1/z^2$ and obtain the Laurent series about 0 for $z \longrightarrow 1/(\sin(z^2))$ which converges on a punctured disc centre 0. But fortunately we are interested only in the first few terms of the Laurent series, those involving powers of $1/z$, so it is sufficient to write

$$(1 + z^4\phi(z))^{-1} = 1 + z^4\psi(z),$$

where we know that $\psi(z)$ is a power series. Thus

$$\frac{1}{\sin(z^2)} = \frac{1}{z^2} + z^2\psi(z).$$

The function has a pole at 0 of order 2, since the Laurent series begins with $1/z^2$. Since no term in $1/z$ occurs,

$$\int_C \frac{1}{\sin(\zeta^2)}\, d\zeta = 0.$$

The art of doing these calculations with economy lies in working out what not to write down.

It is worth while looking at the Laurent series of rational functions in more detail. The singularities of a rational function can be at worst poles (in other words a rational function cannot have an essential singularity; see Problem 4 of Section 8.2). The calculation of the Laurent series of a rational function about a particular singularity is considerably simplified if the function is put into partial fractions. (You will remember the use of partial fractions in real analysis; they are frequently used in integrating rational functions, for example. Partial fractions are discussed in Chapter 18 of **Spivak**. Partial fraction decompositions of complex rational functions are very similar, but simpler in one important respect: since all polynomials factorize into linear factors, we do not have to worry about the quadratic factors that complicate the real case.) For example: the function $z \longrightarrow 1/(z^2 + 1)$ has singularities at $\pm i$. We may write $1/(z^2 + 1)$ in partial fractions as follows:

$$\frac{1}{z^2 + 1} = \frac{1}{(z + i)(z - i)}$$

$$= \frac{A}{z + i} + \frac{B}{z - i}$$

for some complex numbers A and B, which we have to calculate. If we multiply up by $z^2 + 1$, we obtain

$$1 = A(z - i) + B(z + i).$$

There are at least two ways of carrying on from here: either consider particular values of z; or equate coefficients of z and constant terms, giving a pair of simultaneous equations for A and B. Either way, the answers are $A = i/2$, $B = -i/2$, and so

$$\frac{1}{z^2 + 1} = \frac{i}{2} \cdot \frac{1}{z + i} - \frac{i}{2} \cdot \frac{1}{z - i}.$$

If we wish to find the Laurent series of $z \longrightarrow 1/(z^2 + 1)$ about the singularity $-i$, we note that the function $z \longrightarrow 1/(z - i)$ is analytic on a disc centre $-i$ of suitable radius, and so may be expanded in a Taylor series about $-i$. In fact

$$\frac{1}{z - i} = \frac{1}{(z + i) - 2i}$$

$$= \frac{i}{2} \left(1 - \frac{z + i}{2i} \right)^{-1}$$

$$= \frac{i}{2} \left[1 + \left(\frac{z + i}{2i} \right) + \left(\frac{z + i}{2i} \right)^2 + \cdots \right]$$

provided $\left| \dfrac{z + i}{2i} \right| < 1$, that is, provided $|z + i| < 2$.

So

$$\frac{1}{z^2 + 1} = \frac{i}{2} \cdot \frac{1}{z + i} + \frac{1}{4} \left[1 + \left(\frac{z + i}{2i} \right) + \left(\frac{z + i}{2i} \right)^2 + \cdots \right].$$

The details of the calculation are not too important at this stage. The point to notice is that the part of the Laurent series which involves negative powers of $(z + i)$ stands out clearly in the partial fraction decomposition; it is the term $\dfrac{i}{2} \cdot \dfrac{1}{z + i}$. Equally, if we want to find the Laurent series about the singularity $+i$, we can see immediately from the partial fraction decomposition that the part of the series which involves negative powers of $z - i$ is just $-\dfrac{i}{2} \cdot \dfrac{1}{z - i}$.

This is because the function $z \longrightarrow \dfrac{1}{z + i}$ is analytic on a disc centre i of suitable radius.

So we have a method of calculating the Laurent series of a rational function about a singularity α which identifies very simply that part of the series which involves negative powers of $(z - \alpha)$. It will be useful to have a name for this part of the series. We call it the *singular part*, for obvious reasons. (The term *principal part* is used for the same thing by some authors.)

Definition

Suppose that f has a pole of order m at α, and that

$$f(z) = \sum_{n = -m}^{\infty} a_n (z - \alpha)^n, \quad z \neq \alpha,$$

is the Laurent series for f about α. We call the function

$$z \longrightarrow \frac{a_{-m}}{(z - \alpha)^m} + \frac{a_{-m+1}}{(z - \alpha)^{m-1}} + \cdots + \frac{a_{-1}}{z - \alpha}, \quad z \neq \alpha,$$

that is,

$$z \longrightarrow \sum_{n = -m}^{-1} a_n (z - \alpha)^n, \quad z \neq \alpha,$$

the **singular part** of f at α.

Our previous example concerned a function with simple poles; if the singularity in question is a pole of order more than 1, things become a little more complicated. Another complication occurs if the degree of the numerator of the rational function is not less than the degree of the denominator. The following example should clear things up.

Example 4

Find the singular part of the function

$$z \longrightarrow \frac{z^4 + z^3 + z^2 + 3z}{(z - 1)(z + 1)^2}$$

at the point -1.

Solution

We must first of all write $\dfrac{z^4 + z^3 + z^2 + 3z}{(z - 1)(z + 1)^2}$ in the form of a polynomial plus a rational function for which the degree of the numerator is less than the degree of the denominator. Now

$$(z - 1)(z + 1)^2 = z^3 + z^2 - z - 1,$$

so, by long division,

$$\frac{z^4 + z^3 + z^2 + 3z}{(z - 1)(z + 1)^2} = z + \frac{2z^2 + 4z}{(z - 1)(z + 1)^2}.$$

The first term on the right is entire. Since we are concerned only with the singular part of the rational function, we may as well ignore z. It is necessary next to put $\dfrac{2z^2 + 4z}{(z - 1)(z + 1)^2}$ into partial fractions. There are in common use two ways of setting about this. We could express $\dfrac{2z^2 + 4z}{(z - 1)(z + 1)^2}$ in partial fractions in the following form:

$$\frac{2z^2 + 4z}{(z - 1)(z + 1)^2} = \frac{A}{z - 1} + \frac{Bz + C}{(z + 1)^2},$$

where A, B and C are as yet unknown complex numbers. It is also possible to use this form of partial fraction decomposition:

$$\frac{2z^2 + 4z}{(z - 1)(z + 1)^2} = \frac{D}{z - 1} + \frac{E}{z + 1} + \frac{F}{(z + 1)^2}.$$

Evidently the second form is better for our purposes since the two terms involving $z + 1$ on the right are just like terms of a Laurent series. The term $D/(z - 1)$ is ignored. The usual kind of calculation gives

$$E = \tfrac{1}{2}, \qquad F = 1, \quad \text{and} \quad D = \tfrac{3}{2} \text{ (although we do not need it)}.$$

The singular part of $z \longrightarrow \dfrac{z^4 + z^3 + z^2 + 3z}{(z - 1)(z + 1)^2}$ at -1 is thus

$$z \longrightarrow \frac{1}{2} \cdot \frac{1}{(z + 1)} + \frac{1}{(z + 1)^2}.$$

Summary

If a function f has a pole of order m at α, it may be expressed as a Laurent series about α

$$f(z) = \sum_{n=-m}^{\infty} a_n(z - \alpha)^n,$$

which converges on a punctured disc centre α. The series is uniquely determined, the coefficients being given by the formulas

$$a_n = \frac{1}{2\pi i} \int_C \frac{f(\zeta)}{(\zeta - \alpha)^{n+1}} d\zeta, \quad n \geqslant -m.$$

Laurent series are usually found by indirect means, from known Taylor series. This gives a method for computing certain integrals without doing any integration.

If f is a rational function, one useful way of calculating at least the singular part of its Laurent series is to put it into partial fractions.

Self-Assessment Questions

1. To which of the following functions may we apply the results of this section, to find a Laurent series about 0?

   $$z \longrightarrow \frac{\sin(z^2)}{z^m}, m \geqslant 1;$$

   $$z \longrightarrow \exp(1/z^2);$$

   $$z \longrightarrow \frac{1}{z(z - 1)}.$$

2. What is the order of the pole of $z \longrightarrow \dfrac{\sin(z^2)}{z^m}$ at 0, where $m \geqslant 3$? Find

   $\displaystyle\int_C \frac{\sin(\zeta^2)}{\zeta^m} d\zeta$ where C is the circle $|\zeta| = 1$.

3. Find the Laurent series for $z \longrightarrow \dfrac{1}{z(z - 1)}$

   (i) about 0, convergent on the punctured disc $0 < |z| < 1$.

   (ii) about 1, convergent on the punctured disc $0 < |z - 1| < 1$.

Solutions

1.   The function $z \longrightarrow \exp(1/z^2)$ has an essential singularity at 0, so the results of this section cannot be applied to it. (We shall investigate Laurent series for such functions in Section 8.7.) The other functions pass muster—though if $m = 1$ or 2, the singularity of $z \longrightarrow \dfrac{\sin(z^2)}{z^m}$ at 0 is removable, so we are really dealing with Taylor series.

2. $$\frac{\sin(z^2)}{z^m} = \frac{1}{z^m}\left(z^2 - \frac{z^6}{3!} + \frac{z^{10}}{5!} - \frac{z^{14}}{7!} + \cdots\right).$$

The singularity is a pole of order $m - 2$, if $m \geqslant 3$. If m is of the form $4k + 3$, $k \geqslant 0$, the coefficient of $\dfrac{1}{z}$ is $\dfrac{(-1)^k}{(2k+1)!}$, and so

$$\int_C \frac{\sin(\zeta^2)}{\zeta^m}\, d\zeta = 2\pi i \cdot \frac{(-1)^k}{(2k+1)!}.$$

Otherwise the coefficient is 0, and so is the integral.

3. $$\frac{1}{z(z-1)} = -\frac{1}{z} + \frac{1}{z-1} = -\frac{1}{z} - \frac{1}{1-z}.$$

(i)   The Laurent series for $z \longrightarrow \dfrac{1}{z(z-1)}$ about 0 is

$$-\frac{1}{z} - 1 - z - z^2 - z^3 - \cdots,$$

which is convergent on the punctured disc $0 < |z| < 1$.

(ii)   The Laurent series for $z \longrightarrow \dfrac{1}{z(z-1)}$ about 1 is

$$\frac{1}{z-1} - 1 + (z-1) - (z-1)^2 + (z-1)^3 - \cdots,$$

which is convergent on the punctured disc $0 < |z-1| < 1$.

8.6 PROBLEMS

1. Find the first four terms of Laurent series for the following functions about the specified points.

    (i) $z \longrightarrow \dfrac{\cos z}{z^2}$,   about 0.

    (ii) $z \longrightarrow \dfrac{1}{(1-z)(2-z)}$,   about 1.

    (iii) $z \longrightarrow \dfrac{1}{z^2(z^2+1)}$,   about 0.

    (iv) $z \longrightarrow \dfrac{1}{z^2(z^2+1)}$,   about i.

    (v) $z \longrightarrow \dfrac{1}{z}\left(\dfrac{1}{z}-1\right)\left(\dfrac{1}{z}-2\right)$,   about 0.

2. Find the singular parts of the following functions at 0 and, where appropriate, give the order of the pole at 0.

    (i) $z \longrightarrow \cot z$ (Note: $\cot = \cos/\sin$.)

    (ii) $z \longrightarrow \dfrac{1}{e^z - 1}$.

    (iii) $z \longrightarrow \dfrac{(e^z - 1)^2}{z^2}$.

    (iv) $z \longrightarrow \dfrac{e^{iz}}{(z^2 + 1)^2}$.

3. Calculate the following integrals, where C is the circle $|z| = 1$. (Hint: Use the results of Problem 2.)

    (i) $\displaystyle\int_C \cot\zeta \, d\zeta$.

    (ii) $\displaystyle\int_C \dfrac{1}{e^\zeta - 1} \, d\zeta$.

    (iii) $\displaystyle\int_C \dfrac{(e^\zeta - 1)^2}{\zeta^2} \, d\zeta$.

    (iv) $\displaystyle\int_C \dfrac{e^{i\zeta}}{(\zeta^2 + 2)^2} \, d\zeta$.

4. The result of this problem will be used in the next problem and later.

    We say that $\lim\limits_{z \to \infty} f(z) = 0$ if the domain of f contains the set $\{z : |z| > r\}$ for some positive r, and if given $\varepsilon > 0$ there is some real number $N > 0$ such that $|f(z)| < \varepsilon$ whenever $|z| > N$.

    (i)   Show that $\lim\limits_{z \to \infty} f(z) = 0$ if and only if $\lim\limits_{z \to 0} f(1/z) = 0$. (You may recall that this kind of limit was introduced in Section 5.7 of *Unit 5*. This part of the question asks you to prove something which was stated there.)

    (ii) Show that if $\lim\limits_{z \to \infty} f(z) = \lim\limits_{z \to \infty} g(z) = 0$, then $\lim\limits_{z \to \infty} (f + g)(z) = 0$.

    (iii) Show that $\lim\limits_{z \to \infty} \dfrac{1}{(z - \alpha)^n} = 0$, when $n \geqslant 1$.

    (iv) Show that if f is entire and $\lim\limits_{z \to \infty} f(z) = 0$, then $f = 0$. (Hint: Liouville's Theorem.)

5. Show that if f is entire and $z \longrightarrow f(1/z)$ has a pole at 0 then f is a polynomial. Deduce that $z \longrightarrow \sin(1/z)$ has an essential singularity at 0.

6. Show that if f has a finite number of poles, and no other singularities, and if $z \longrightarrow f(1/z)$ has a pole at 0, then f is a rational function.

Solutions

1. (i) Since $\cos z = 1 - \dfrac{z^2}{2!} + \dfrac{z^4}{4!} - \dfrac{z^6}{6!} + \cdots$, for any z,

$$\frac{\cos z}{z^2} = \frac{1}{z^2} - \frac{1}{2!} + \frac{z^2}{4!} - \frac{z^4}{6!} + \cdots, \quad z \neq 0.$$

(ii) $$\frac{1}{(1-z)(2-z)} = \frac{1}{1-z} - \frac{1}{2-z}$$

$$= -\frac{1}{z-1} - \frac{1}{1-(z-1)}$$

$$= -\frac{1}{z-1} - 1 - (z-1) - (z-1)^2 - \cdots,$$

provided $0 < |z-1| < 1$.

(iii) $$\frac{1}{z^2(z^2+1)} = \frac{1}{z^2(z+i)(z-i)}$$

$$= \frac{1}{z^2} - \frac{i}{2(z+i)} + \frac{i}{2(z-i)}.$$

To obtain the Laurent series about 0, we expand $\dfrac{1}{z+i}$ and $\dfrac{1}{z-i}$ in powers of z:

$$\frac{1}{z+i} = -\frac{i}{1-iz} = -i(1 + iz + (iz)^2 + (iz)^3 + \cdots)$$

and

$$\frac{1}{z-i} = \frac{i}{1+iz} = i(1 - iz + (iz)^2 - (iz)^3 + \cdots).$$

These series both converge for $|z| < 1$. Thus if $0 < |z| < 1$,

$$\frac{1}{z^2(z^2+1)} = \frac{1}{z^2} + \frac{1}{2}(1 + iz + (iz)^2 + (iz)^3 + \cdots)$$

$$- \frac{1}{2}(1 - iz + (iz)^2 - (iz)^3 + \cdots)$$

$$= \frac{1}{z^2} + iz + (iz)^3 + (iz)^5 + \cdots.$$

(iv) In (iii) we had

$$\frac{1}{z^2(z^2+1)} = \frac{1}{z^2} - \frac{i}{2(z+i)} + \frac{i}{2(z-i)}.$$

To obtain the Laurent series about i we have to expand $\dfrac{1}{z^2}$ and $\dfrac{1}{z+i}$ in powers of $(z-i)$. Now $z = i(1 - i(z-i))$, so that

$$\frac{1}{z^2} = \frac{1}{[i(1-i(z-i))]^2} = -\frac{1}{(1-i(z-i))^2}$$

$$= -(1 - 2i(z-i) + 3(i(z-i))^2 + \cdots)$$

provided $|z-i| < 1$. Also,

$$\frac{1}{z+i} = \frac{1}{2i\left(1 - \frac{i}{2}(z-i)\right)}$$

$$= \frac{1}{2i}\left(1 + \frac{i}{2}(z-i) + \left(\frac{i}{2}(z-i)\right)^2 + \cdots\right),$$

provided $|z - i| < 2$. Thus if $0 < |z - i| < 1$,

$$\frac{1}{z^2(z^2+1)} = -1 + 2i(z-i) - 3(i(z-i))^2 + \cdots$$

$$-\frac{1}{4}\left(1 + \frac{i}{2}(z-i) + \left(\frac{i}{2}(z-i)\right)^2 + \cdots\right)$$

$$+ \frac{i}{2(z-i)}$$

$$= \frac{i}{2(z-i)} - \frac{5}{4} + \frac{15}{8}i(z-i) + \frac{49}{16}(z-i)^2 + \cdots.$$

(v)   Since $\frac{1}{z}\left(\frac{1}{z} - 1\right)\left(\frac{1}{z} - 2\right) = \frac{1}{z^3} - \frac{3}{z^2} + \frac{2}{z}$, the Laurent series is just $\frac{1}{z^3} - \frac{3}{z^2} + \frac{2}{z}$.

2.   (i) $\cot z = \dfrac{\cos z}{\sin z} = \left(1 - \dfrac{z^2}{2!} + \cdots\right) \cdot \dfrac{1}{z}\left(1 - \dfrac{z^2}{3!} + \cdots\right)^{-1}$

$$= \frac{1}{z}\left(1 - \frac{z^2}{2!} + \cdots\right) \cdot \left(1 + \frac{z^2}{3!} + \cdots\right)$$

$$= \frac{1}{z} - \frac{1}{3}z + \text{terms in positive powers of } z.$$

The singular part is thus $z \longrightarrow 1/z$, and the function has a simple pole.

(ii) $\dfrac{1}{e^z - 1} = \left(z + \dfrac{z^2}{2!} + \dfrac{z^3}{3!} + \cdots\right)^{-1}$

$$= \frac{1}{z}\left(1 + \frac{z}{2!} + \frac{z^2}{3!} + \cdots\right)^{-1}$$

$$= \frac{1}{z}\left(1 - \left(\frac{z}{2!} + \frac{z^2}{3!} + \cdots\right) + \cdots\right).$$

$$= \frac{1}{z} - \frac{1}{2} + \text{terms in positive powers of } z.$$

The singular part is thus $z \longrightarrow 1/z$, and the function has a simple pole.

(iii) $\dfrac{(e^z - 1)^2}{z^2} = \dfrac{1}{z^2}\left(z + \dfrac{z^2}{2!} + \dfrac{z^3}{3!} + \cdots\right)^2$

$$= \frac{1}{z^2} \cdot z^2\left(1 + \frac{z}{2!} + \frac{z^2}{3!} + \cdots\right)^2$$

$$= \left(1 + \frac{z}{2!} + \frac{z^2}{3!} + \cdots\right)^2$$

$$= 1 + z + \text{terms in positive powers of } z.$$

So the singular part is the zero function, and the function has a removable singularity at 0.

(iv)   This function is evidently analytic on some neighbourhood of 0, that is, its singular part is the zero function and the function has no singularity at 0.

3.   The first two integrals may be evaluated using the rule that the coefficient of $\dfrac{1}{z}$ in the Laurent series for f is $\dfrac{1}{2\pi i}\displaystyle\int_C f(\zeta)\,d\zeta$, where C is a suitable circle centre 0 (for example, the circle $|z| = 1$). We have already calculated the appropriate coefficients in Problem 2. We obtain

(i) $\displaystyle\int_C \cot\zeta \, d\zeta = 2\pi i;$

(ii) $\displaystyle\int_C \frac{1}{e^\zeta - 1}\, d\zeta = 2\pi i.$

The other two integrals are both 0, by Cauchy's Theorem.

4. (i) Suppose that $\lim_{z \to \infty} f(z) = 0$. Then there is some N such that $|f(z)| < \varepsilon$ whenever $|z| > N$. But then $|f(1/z)| < \varepsilon$ whenever $|1/z| > N$ and $z \neq 0$, that is, whenever $0 < |z| < 1/N$. Thus $\lim_{z \to 0} f(1/z) = 0$.

Suppose that $\lim_{z \to 0} f(1/z) = 0$. Then there is some $\delta > 0$ such that $|f(1/z)| < \varepsilon$ whenever $0 < |z| < \delta$. But then $|f(z)| < \varepsilon$ whenever $0 < |1/z| < \delta$, that is, whenever $|z| > 1/\delta$. Thus $\lim_{z \to \infty} f(z) = 0$.

(ii) This follows immediately from the triangle inequality.

(iii) Given $\varepsilon > 0$, let $N = |\alpha| + (1/\varepsilon)^{1/n}$. Then if $|z| > N$, we have

$$|z - \alpha| \geq ||z| - |\alpha|| > (1/\varepsilon)^{1/n},$$

and so

$$\frac{1}{|z - \alpha|^n} < \varepsilon.$$

Thus, $\lim_{z \to \infty} \frac{1}{(z - \alpha)^n} = 0$.

(iv) We show that if $\lim_{z \to \infty} f(z) = 0$ then f is bounded. There is some N such that $|f(z)| < 1$ when $|z| > N$. But f is entire, and so continuous, and so, in particular, continuous on the closed disc $|z| \leq N$. Thus it is bounded on the disc $|z| \leq N$: say $|f(z)| \leq K$. Then $|f(z)| \leq \max(1, K)$ for all z. Now by Liouville's Theorem f is constant; and since $\lim_{z \to \infty} f(z) = 0$, the constant can be only 0.

5. Let $f(1/z) = \frac{a_{-m}}{z^m} + \cdots + \frac{a_{-1}}{z} + a_0 + z\phi(z)$, where ϕ is entire. Then $f(z) = a_{-m}z^m + \cdots + a_{-1}z + a_0 + \frac{1}{z}\phi(1/z)$. Since f is entire, $z \longrightarrow \frac{1}{z}\phi(1/z)$ is entire; moreover $|\phi(z)|$ is bounded for $|z| < 1$, say, so $|\phi(1/z)|$ is bounded for $|z| \geq 1$. Thus $\lim_{z \to \infty} \frac{1}{z}\phi(1/z) = 0$, and so by Problem 4, $z \longrightarrow \frac{1}{z}\phi(1/z)$ is the zero function. Thus $f(z) = a_{-m}z^m + \cdots + a_1 z + a_0$ is a polynomial.

Since sin is entire and it is not a polynomial, $z \longrightarrow \sin 1/z$ cannot have a pole at 0. The singularity of $z \longrightarrow \sin 1/z$ at zero is certainly not removable: so $z \longrightarrow \sin 1/z$ has an essential singularity at 0.

6. Suppose that f has poles at $\alpha_1, \alpha_2, \ldots, \alpha_n$, and that the singular parts of f at these points are $\phi_1, \phi_2, \ldots, \phi_n$. Consider the function $f - \phi_1 - \phi_2 - \cdots - \phi_n$. It also has singularities at $\alpha_1, \alpha_2, \ldots, \alpha_n$, but they are removable. To see this, consider, for example, the point α_1. There is a neighbourhood of α_1 on which $\phi_2, \phi_3, \ldots, \phi_n$ are analytic. The function $f - \phi_1$ is represented by a power series on a suitable punctured disc about α_1; but this power series must converge, to an analytic function, on the whole disc. Thus, α_1 is a removable singularity of $f - \phi_1$, and so a removable singularity of $f - \phi_1 - \phi_2 - \cdots - \phi_n$. A similar argument applies to the points $\alpha_2, \ldots, \alpha_n$. Let g be the function obtained from $f - \phi_1 - \phi_2 - \cdots - \phi_n$ by removing its singularities. Then g is entire. Now the functions $z \longrightarrow \phi_1(1/z)$, $z \longrightarrow \phi_2(1/z), \ldots$, $z \longrightarrow \phi_n(1/z)$ have poles (or possibly removable singularities) at 0 since they are rational functions, whereas $z \longrightarrow f(1/z)$ has a pole at 0 by hypothesis. Thus $z \longrightarrow g(1/z)$ has a pole at 0, and so by Problem 5 above, g is a polynomial. Thus

$$f = g + \phi_1 + \phi_2 + \cdots + \phi_n \quad \text{on } \mathbf{C} - \{\alpha_1, \alpha_2, \ldots, \alpha_n\},$$

where g is a polynomial and $\phi_1, \phi_2, \ldots, \phi_n$ are rational. This means that f is rational.

8.7   LAURENT SERIES: GENERAL CASE

The function $z \longrightarrow \exp 1/z$ may be expanded in a Laurent series: since $1+z+\dfrac{z^2}{2!}+\dfrac{z^3}{3!}+\cdots$ converges to $\exp z$ for all z, the series $1+\dfrac{1}{z}+\dfrac{1}{2!}\cdot\dfrac{1}{z^2}+\dfrac{1}{3!}\cdot\dfrac{1}{z^3}+\cdots$ converges to $\exp 1/z$ whenever $z \neq 0$. There is an obvious difference between this Laurent series and the ones we dealt with in Section 8.5, namely that it involves *all* negative powers of z, rather than only finitely many. Here is another consequence of the fact that the singularity of $z \longrightarrow \exp 1/z$ at 0 is essential.

In general we cannot expect that the Laurent series for a function about an essential singularity α will contain only non-positive powers of $(z - \alpha)$. We shall have to discuss series which extend to infinity in both directions; fortunately this does not really create any new problems, because we can consider such a series as the sum of two ordinary series, one containing the negative powers of $(z - \alpha)$ and the other the non-negative powers.

Definition

If both the series $\displaystyle\sum_{n=0}^{\infty} a_n(z - \alpha)^n$ and $\displaystyle\sum_{n=1}^{\infty} \frac{a_{-n}}{(z - \alpha)^n}$ converge, we say that

$\displaystyle\sum_{n=-\infty}^{\infty} a_n(z - \alpha)^n$ **converges**, and that its **sum** is $\displaystyle\sum_{n=0}^{\infty} a_n(z - \alpha)^n + \sum_{n=1}^{\infty} \frac{a_{-n}}{(z - \alpha)^n}$.

We usually break a Laurent series to the left of the constant term, as in the definition; but it does not matter really where the break is made, since the addition or subtraction of a finite number of terms does not affect the convergence of a series.

We next prove the existence and uniqueness of the Laurent series for a function about an essential singularity. The formulation of this result is very similar to that of Theorem 6, in which we proved the corresponding result for poles, and which is a special case of the new theorem. We cannot use the same sort of simple argument, though; instead we adapt the proof of the existence of the Taylor series, Theorem 9, of *Unit 6*, and make use of Theorem 2 (page 13)

Theorem 7

Suppose that f is analytic on the punctured disc $0 < |z - \alpha| < r$. Let $a_n = \dfrac{1}{2\pi i} \displaystyle\int_C \frac{f(\zeta)}{(\zeta - \alpha)^{n+1}} d\zeta, n \in \mathbf{Z}$ (the set of positive and negative integers and zero), where C is a circle $|\zeta - \alpha| = \rho$, with $0 < \rho < r$. Then (i) the series $\displaystyle\sum_{n=-\infty}^{\infty} a_n(z - \alpha)^n$ converges for $0 < |z - \alpha| < r$, and its sum is $f(z)$. Moreover, (ii) this representation of f by a Laurent series about α is unique: that is, if a series $\displaystyle\sum_{n=-\infty}^{\infty} b_n(z - \alpha)^n$ also converges to $f(z)$ on the punctured disc $0 < |z - \alpha| < r$, then $b_n = a_n$ for all $n \in \mathbf{Z}$.

Proof

(i)   Let z be a point in the punctured disc, so that $0 < |z - \alpha| < r$; let ρ_1, ρ_2 be real numbers such that $0 < \rho_1 < |z - \alpha| < \rho_2 < r$, and let C_1, C_2 be the circles $|\zeta - \alpha| = \rho_1$ and $|\zeta - \alpha| = \rho_2$ respectively. See Fig. 7.

Then by Cauchy's Formula for a punctured disc, Theorem 2,

$$f(z) = \frac{1}{2\pi i} \int_{C_2} \frac{f(\zeta)}{\zeta - z} d\zeta - \frac{1}{2\pi i} \int_{C_1} \frac{f(\zeta)}{\zeta - z} d\zeta.$$

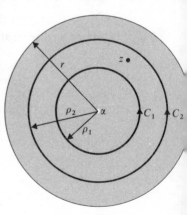

Fig. 7

We show that the part of the Laurent series containing non-negative powers of $(z - \alpha)$ converges to the first of these two integrals in exactly the same way that we proved Theorem 9 of *Unit 6*. Indeed, since the arguments are so similar we do not think it necessary to give the full details of this part of the proof.

The calculation uses the formula for the sum of a finite geometric series in the form

$$\frac{1}{1 - \lambda} = 1 + \lambda + \lambda^2 + \cdots + \lambda^N + \frac{\lambda^{N+1}}{1 - \lambda}$$

$$= \sum_{n=0}^{N} \lambda^n + \frac{\lambda^{N+1}}{1 - \lambda}.$$

This formula holds for any complex number λ other than 1 and any positive integer N. Now

$$\frac{1}{\zeta - z} = \frac{1}{(\zeta - \alpha) - (z - \alpha)} = \frac{1}{\zeta - \alpha} \cdot \frac{1}{1 - \left(\dfrac{z - \alpha}{\zeta - \alpha}\right)}.$$

Using the formula, with $\left(\dfrac{z - \alpha}{\zeta - \alpha}\right)$ in place of λ, we obtain

$$\frac{1}{\zeta - z} = \frac{1}{\zeta - \alpha} \left(\sum_{n=0}^{N} \left(\frac{z - \alpha}{\zeta - \alpha}\right)^n + \left(\frac{z - \alpha}{\zeta - \alpha}\right)^{N+1} \cdot \frac{1}{1 - \left(\dfrac{z - \alpha}{\zeta - \alpha}\right)} \right)$$

$$= \sum_{n=0}^{N} \frac{(z - \alpha)^n}{(\zeta - \alpha)^{n+1}} + \frac{(z - \alpha)^{N+1}}{(\zeta - \alpha)^{N+1}(\zeta - z)}.$$

Thus, multiplying by $\dfrac{f(\zeta)}{2\pi i}$ and integrating along C_2, we obtain

$$\frac{1}{2\pi i} \int_{C_2} \frac{f(\zeta)}{\zeta - z} \, d\zeta = \sum_{n=0}^{N} \left((z - \alpha)^n \cdot \frac{1}{2\pi i} \int_{C_2} \frac{f(\zeta)}{(\zeta - \alpha)^{n+1}} \, d\zeta \right)$$

$$+ (z - \alpha)^{N+1} \cdot \frac{1}{2\pi i} \int_{C_2} \frac{f(\zeta)}{(\zeta - \alpha)^{N+1}(\zeta - z)} \, d\zeta.$$

(*Note*: Throughout this part of the proof, terms on a tone background will be shown to approach zero.)

By the deformation lemma of *Unit 5* (page 75)

$$\frac{1}{2\pi i} \int_{C_2} \frac{f(\zeta)}{(\zeta - \alpha)^{n+1}} \, d\zeta = \frac{1}{2\pi i} \int_{C} \frac{f(\zeta)}{(\zeta - \alpha)^{n+1}} \, d\zeta = a_n.$$

Thus

$$\frac{1}{2\pi i} \int_{C_2} \frac{f(\zeta)}{\zeta - z} \, d\zeta = \sum_{n=0}^{N} a_n (z - \alpha)^n$$

$$+ (z - \alpha)^{N+1} \cdot \frac{1}{2\pi i} \int_{C_2} \frac{f(\zeta)}{(\zeta - \alpha)^{N+1}(\zeta - z)} \, d\zeta.$$

To show that the series $\displaystyle\sum_{n=0}^{\infty} a_n (z - \alpha)^n$ converges to $\dfrac{1}{2\pi i} \displaystyle\int_{C_2} \frac{f(\zeta)}{\zeta - z} \, d\zeta$ we have to show that

$$\lim_{N \to \infty} \left((z - \alpha)^{N+1} \cdot \frac{1}{2\pi i} \int_{C_2} \frac{f(\zeta)}{(\zeta - \alpha)^{N+1}(\zeta - z)} \, d\zeta \right) = 0.$$

This is done by estimating the integral in the usual way. Since a very similar argument is used in the proof of Theorem 9 of *Unit 6*, and we are in any case going to use just such an argument later in this proof, we do not propose to give the details, but merely to state that $\sum_{n=0}^{\infty} a_n(z - \alpha)^n$ does in fact converge to $\dfrac{1}{2\pi i}\displaystyle\int_{C_2} \dfrac{f(\zeta)}{\zeta - z}\,d\zeta$.

In this part of the proof we chose to express everything in terms of $\dfrac{z - \alpha}{\zeta - \alpha}$ because z lies inside C_2 and so $\left|\dfrac{z - \alpha}{\zeta - \alpha}\right| < 1$ when ζ lies on C_2. It is this that makes the above limit 0. Since z lies outside C_1, the obvious thing to do to deal with the integral over C_1 is to try to express everything in terms of $\dfrac{\zeta - \alpha}{z - \alpha}$ instead.

This we can easily do, as follows. We write

$$\frac{1}{\zeta - z} = \frac{1}{(\zeta - \alpha) - (z - \alpha)} = \frac{1}{z - \alpha} \cdot \frac{1}{\left(\dfrac{\zeta - \alpha}{z - \alpha}\right) - 1};$$

using the formula for a geometric series with $\left(\dfrac{\zeta - \alpha}{z - \alpha}\right)$ for λ, we have

$$\frac{1}{\zeta - z} = -\frac{1}{z - \alpha} \cdot \left(\sum_{n=0}^{N} \left(\frac{\zeta - \alpha}{z - \alpha}\right)^n + \left(\frac{\zeta - \alpha}{z - \alpha}\right)^{N+1} \cdot \frac{1}{1 - \left(\dfrac{\zeta - \alpha}{z - \alpha}\right)}\right)$$

$$= -\sum_{n=0}^{N} \frac{(\zeta - \alpha)^n}{(z - \alpha)^{n+1}} - \frac{(\zeta - \alpha)^{N+1}}{(z - \alpha)^{N+1}(z - \zeta)}.$$

Thus

$$-\frac{1}{2\pi i}\int_{C_1} \frac{f(\zeta)}{\zeta - z}\,d\zeta = \sum_{n=0}^{N} \left(\frac{1}{(z - \alpha)^{n+1}} \cdot \frac{1}{2\pi i}\int_{C_1} f(\zeta)(\zeta - \alpha)^n\,d\zeta\right)$$

$$+ \frac{1}{(z - \alpha)^{N+1}} \cdot \frac{1}{2\pi i}\int_{C_1} \frac{f(\zeta)(\zeta - \alpha)^{N+1}}{(z - \zeta)}\,d\zeta.$$

By the deformation lemma of *Unit 5* again,

$$\frac{1}{2\pi i}\int_{C_1} f(\zeta)(\zeta - \alpha)^n\,d\zeta = \frac{1}{2\pi i}\int_{C} f(\zeta)(\zeta - \alpha)^n\,d\zeta$$

$$= \frac{1}{2\pi i}\int_{C} \frac{f(\zeta)}{(\zeta - \alpha)^{-n}}\,d\zeta = a_{-(n+1)}.$$

Thus

$$-\frac{1}{2\pi i}\int_{C} \frac{f(\zeta)}{\zeta - z}\,d\zeta = \sum_{n=0}^{N} \frac{a_{-(n+1)}}{(z - \alpha)^{n+1}}$$

$$+ \frac{1}{(z - \alpha)^{N+1}} \cdot \frac{1}{2\pi i}\int_{C_1} \frac{f(\zeta)(\zeta - \alpha)^{N+1}}{(z - \zeta)}\,d\zeta$$

$$= \sum_{n=1}^{N+1} \frac{a_{-n}}{(z - \alpha)^n}$$

$$+ \frac{1}{(z - \alpha)^{N+1}} \cdot \frac{1}{2\pi i}\int_{C_1} \frac{f(\zeta)(\zeta - \alpha)^{N+1}}{(z - \zeta)}\,d\zeta.$$

It remains to be shown that the remainder term—the last term on the right—approaches 0 as N increases. Now f is continuous on C_1, and so bounded: let us suppose that $|f(\zeta)| \leqslant K$ for ζ on C_1.

Also

$$|z - \zeta| \geqslant |z - \alpha| - \rho_1 > 0$$

for ζ on C_1 (Fig. 8).

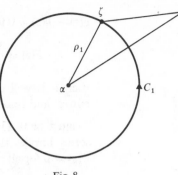

Fig. 8

Thus, by the Estimation Theorem,

$$\left| \frac{1}{2\pi i} \int_{C_1} \frac{f(\zeta)(\zeta - \alpha)^{N+1}}{(z - \zeta)} \, d\zeta \right| \leqslant \frac{1}{2\pi} \int_{C_1} \frac{|f(\zeta)| \cdot |\zeta - \alpha|^{N+1}}{|z - \zeta|} \cdot |d\zeta|$$

$$\leqslant \frac{1}{2\pi} \cdot K \cdot \rho_1^{N+1} \cdot \frac{1}{|z - \alpha| - \rho_1} \cdot 2\pi\rho_1$$

$$= \rho_1^{N+1} \cdot \frac{K\rho_1}{|z - \alpha| - \rho_1}.$$

So

$$\left| \frac{1}{(z - \alpha)^{N+1}} \cdot \frac{1}{2\pi i} \int_{C_1} \frac{f(\zeta)(\zeta - \alpha)^{N+1}}{(z - \zeta)} \, d\zeta \right|$$

$$\leqslant \left(\frac{\rho_1}{|z - \alpha|} \right)^{N+1} \cdot \frac{K\rho_1}{|z - \alpha| - \rho_1}.$$

Since $\dfrac{\rho_1}{|z - \alpha|} < 1$, we have $\lim_{N \to \infty} \left(\dfrac{\rho_1}{|z - \alpha|} \right)^{N+1} = 0$, and we deduce that

$$\lim_{N \to \infty} \left(\frac{1}{(z - \alpha)^{N+1}} \cdot \frac{1}{2\pi i} \int_{C_1} \frac{f(\zeta)(\zeta - \alpha)^{N+1}}{(z - \zeta)} \, d\zeta \right) = 0.$$

Thus the series $\displaystyle\sum_{n=1}^{\infty} \frac{a_{-n}}{(z - \alpha)^n}$ converges to $-\dfrac{1}{2\pi i} \int_{C_1} \dfrac{f(\zeta)}{\zeta - z} \, d\zeta$.

Putting together the two halves of the proof, we conclude that for any z such that $0 < |z - \alpha| < r$, the Laurent series $\displaystyle\sum_{n=-\infty}^{\infty} a_n(z - \alpha)^n$ converges to $f(z)$.

(ii) We now turn to the uniqueness of Laurent series. Suppose that $\displaystyle\sum_{n=-\infty}^{\infty} b_n(z - \alpha)^n$ also converges to $f(z)$ on $0 < |z - \alpha| < r$. Then if $c_n = b_n - a_n$, the series $\displaystyle\sum_{n=-\infty}^{\infty} c_n(z - \alpha)^n$ converges to 0 on $0 < |z - \alpha| < r$. Now the part of this series containing positive powers of $(z - \alpha)$, that is, $\displaystyle\sum_{n=0}^{\infty} c_n(z - \alpha)^n$, is a power series. It converges on $0 < |z - \alpha| < r$; it must therefore converge on $|z - \alpha| < r$, and if we set $g(z) = \displaystyle\sum_{n=0}^{\infty} c_n(z - \alpha)^n$, the function g is analytic on $|z - \alpha| < r$. The series $\displaystyle\sum_{n=1}^{\infty} \frac{c_{-n}}{(z - \alpha)^n}$ also converges on $0 < |z - \alpha| < r$, and so the series $\displaystyle\sum_{n=1}^{\infty} c_{-n}w^n$, obtained by replacing $\dfrac{1}{z - \alpha}$ by w, converges on $|w| > \dfrac{1}{r}$. But it, too, is a power series, and so converges on the whole of $\mathbf{C}$ in fact. Thus if $\phi(w) = \displaystyle\sum_{n=1}^{\infty} c_{-n}w^n$, then ϕ is entire; also $\phi(0) = 0$ since the series has no constant term. So if $h(z) = \phi\left(\dfrac{1}{z - \alpha} \right)$ then h is analytic on $\mathbf{C} - \{\alpha\}$, $\lim_{z \to \infty} h(z) = 0$, and $h(z) = \displaystyle\sum_{n=1}^{\infty} \frac{c_{-n}}{(z - \alpha)^n}$. We therefore have functions g and h such that g is analytic on $|z - \alpha| < r$, h is analytic on $\mathbf{C} - \{\alpha\}$, $\lim_{z \to \infty} h(z) = 0$, and

$g(z) + h(z) = 0$ for $0 < |z - \alpha| < r$. If we set

$$F(z) = \begin{cases} g(z), & |z - \alpha| < r \\ -h(z), & |z - \alpha| > 0 \end{cases}$$

then F is well defined (since $g(z) = -h(z)$ for $0 < |z - \alpha| < r$) and it is entire; and since $\lim_{z \to \infty} F(z) = -\lim_{z \to \infty} h(z) = 0$, by Problem 4 of Section 8.6, F must be 0. Thus $g(z) = 0$ if $|z - \alpha| < r$; and the uniqueness of Taylor series implies that $c_n = 0$ when $n \geqslant 0$. Also, $h(z) = 0$ if $z \neq \alpha$, and so $\phi(z) = 0$ for all z; and so for the same reason, $c_n = 0$ when $n < 0$.

We conclude that $b_n = a_n$ for all $n \in \mathbf{Z}$. ∎

(Notice that in the proof of (ii) we have employed an abuse of language: for example, "... converges on $|z - \alpha| < r$ ..." means "... converges on *the disc* $|z - \alpha| < r$ ...".)

Example 1

The function $z \longrightarrow z \sin 1/z$ has an essential singularity at 0 (in contrast to the real function

$$x \longrightarrow \begin{cases} x \sin 1/x, & x \neq 0 \\ 0, & x = 0, \end{cases}$$

which is continuous at 0). Its Laurent series about 0 is

$$z \left(\frac{1}{z} - \frac{1}{3!} \cdot \frac{1}{z^3} + \frac{1}{5!} \cdot \frac{1}{z^5} - \cdots \right)$$

$$= 1 - \frac{1}{3!} \cdot \frac{1}{z^2} + \frac{1}{5!} \cdot \frac{1}{z^4} - \cdots.$$

Notice that since there is no term in $1/z$, if C is a circle centre 0, then

$$\int_C \zeta \sin 1/\zeta \, d\zeta = 0.$$

There are various other tricks that lead to expansion of functions in series which involve negative powers of z and similar terms, and we wish to cover them in this section too. As an example, consider the function $z \longrightarrow \dfrac{1}{1 - z}$. This function is analytic on the disc $|z| < 1$ and its Taylor series is

$$\frac{1}{1 - z} = 1 + z + z^2 + z^3 + \cdots \quad \text{for } |z| < 1.$$

It is also analytic on $\{z : |z| > 1\}$, of course (Fig. 9).

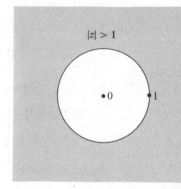

Fig. 9

Can it be expanded in a series in powers of z for $|z| > 1$? It can, in the following way.

$$\frac{1}{1 - z} = -\frac{1}{z} \cdot \frac{1}{1 - \dfrac{1}{z}};$$

if $|z| > 1$, then $|1/z| < 1$, so

$$\frac{1}{1 - z} = -\frac{1}{z} \left(1 + \frac{1}{z} + \frac{1}{z^2} + \cdots \right) = -\frac{1}{z} - \frac{1}{z^2} - \frac{1}{z^3} - \cdots.$$

So again we have a representation of a function as a series involving negative powers of z.

We shall consider one further, and slightly more complicated, example. The function $z \longrightarrow \dfrac{1}{(1 - z)(2 - z)}$ has singularities at 1 and 2. It is therefore analytic on the annulus $1 < |z| < 2$ (Fig. 10), as well as on many other regions, of course.

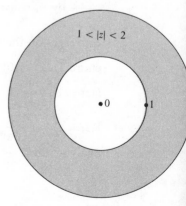

Fig. 10

Now,

$$\frac{1}{(1-z)(2-z)} = \frac{1}{1-z} - \frac{1}{2-z}.$$

The function $z \longrightarrow \dfrac{1}{1-z}$ is analytic on the set $\{z : |z| > 1\}$, and has the Laurent series expansion $-\dfrac{1}{z} - \dfrac{1}{z^2} - \dfrac{1}{z^3} \cdots$ there. The function $z \longrightarrow \dfrac{1}{2-z}$ is analytic on the disc $|z| < 2$, and has the Taylor series expansion $\dfrac{1}{2} + \dfrac{z}{2^2} + \dfrac{z^2}{2^3} + \dfrac{z^3}{2^4} + \cdots$ there. So, using an obvious notation, the series

$$\cdots - \frac{1}{z^3} - \frac{1}{z^2} - \frac{1}{z} - \frac{1}{2} - \frac{z}{2^2} - \frac{z^2}{2^3} - \frac{z^3}{2^4} - \cdots$$

converges to $\dfrac{1}{(1-z)(2-z)}$ provided that $|z| > 1$ *and* $|z| < 2$. It converges, in other words, on the annulus $1 < |z| < 2$.

In fact any function analytic on an annulus has a unique Laurent series, convergent on the annulus, like the one we constructed for the function $z \longrightarrow \dfrac{1}{(1-z)(2-z)}$ on the annulus $1 < |z| < 2$. The word "annulus" is to be interpreted here in not too strict a sense. In the same way that we have been using the phrase "punctured disc" to mean "punctured plane" where appropriate, we shall consider the complement of a closed disc of positive radius r_1 to be kind of annulus, an annulus $r_1 < |z - \alpha| < \infty$. We wish to prove the following theorem which is an obvious generalization of Theorem 7*.

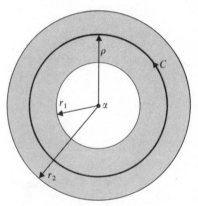

Fig. 11

Theorem 8

Suppose that f is analytic on the annulus $r_1 < |z - \alpha| < r_2$, where $0 < r_1 < r_2$, and r_2 may be infinite. Let $a_n = \dfrac{1}{2\pi i} \displaystyle\int_C \dfrac{f(\zeta)}{(\zeta - \alpha)^{n+1}} \, d\zeta$, $n \in \mathbf{Z}$, where C is a circle $|\zeta - \alpha| = \rho$, with $r_1 < \rho < r_2$. Then (i) the series $\displaystyle\sum_{n=-\infty}^{\infty} a_n (z - \alpha)^n$ converges for $r_1 < |z - \alpha| < r_2$, and its sum is $f(z)$. Moreover, (ii) this representation of f by a Laurent series about α is unique.

The proof of Theorem 8 is in principle the same as the proof of Theorem 7, provided that Cauchy's Formula can be shown to hold for an annulus. That is to say, if it can be shown that

if ρ_1 and ρ_2 are real numbers such that $r_1 < \rho_1 < |z - \alpha| < \rho_2 < r_2$, and C_1 and C_2 are the circles $|\zeta - \alpha| = \rho_1$ and $|\zeta - \alpha| = \rho_2$, respectively, then

$$f(z) = \frac{1}{2\pi i} \int_{C_2} \frac{f(\zeta)}{\zeta - z} \, d\zeta - \frac{1}{2\pi i} \int_{C_1} \frac{f(\zeta)}{\zeta - z} \, d\zeta,$$

then the proof of Theorem 7 requires little adaptation to prove Theorem 8 as well (Fig. 12).

The proof of Cauchy's Formula for an annulus is rather a technical matter, and we shall not consider it until *Unit 9, Cauchy's Theorem II*: see Problem 5 of Section 9.6 there. We ask you to accept for now the truth of the statement above; and as a consequence, the truth of Theorem 8.

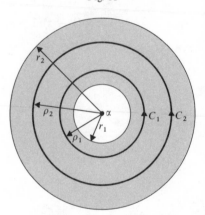

Fig. 12

Example 2

A function may have lots of different Laurent series representations about the same point, but converging on different regions. It is very important to make sure that we calculate the right series. Consider, for example, the function

$$z \longrightarrow \frac{1}{(1-z)(2-z)}.$$

---

* *Pierre Alphonse Laurent* (1813–1854), who was a French military engineer, discovered this result in 1843. The result, however, was already known to Weierstrass.

We calculated its Laurent series about 0 on the annulus $1 < |z| < 2$ (Fig. 13). But we can also find a series representation for this function on the disc $|z| < 1$, on which it is analytic (Fig. 14). This is actually a Taylor series:

$$\frac{1}{(1-z)(2-z)} = \frac{1}{1-z} - \frac{1}{2-z}$$

$$= \frac{1}{1-z} - \frac{1}{2} \cdot \frac{1}{1 - \dfrac{z}{2}}$$

$$= 1 + z + z^2 + \cdots$$

$$\quad - \frac{1}{2}\left(1 + \frac{z}{2} + \left(\frac{z}{2}\right)^2 + \cdots\right)$$

$$\left(\text{since } |z| < 1 \quad \text{and} \quad \left|\frac{z}{2}\right| < \frac{1}{2} < 1\right)$$

$$= \frac{1}{2} + \frac{3}{4}z + \frac{7}{8}z^2 + \cdots.$$

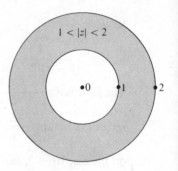

Fig. 13

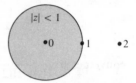

Fig. 14

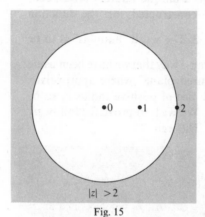

Fig. 15

There is also a series representation which converges on the "annulus" $|z| > 2$ (Fig. 15).

$$\frac{1}{(1-z)(2-z)} = \frac{1}{1-z} - \frac{1}{2-z}$$

$$= -\frac{1}{z} \cdot \frac{1}{1 - \dfrac{1}{z}} + \frac{1}{z} \cdot \frac{1}{1 - \dfrac{2}{z}}$$

$$= -\frac{1}{z}\left(1 + \frac{1}{z} + \frac{1}{z^2} + \cdots\right)$$

$$\quad + \frac{1}{z}\left(1 + \frac{2}{z} + \left(\frac{2}{z}\right)^2 + \cdots\right)$$

$$\left(\text{since } \left|\frac{1}{z}\right| < \frac{1}{2} < 1 \quad \text{and} \quad \left|\frac{2}{z}\right| < 1\right)$$

$$= \frac{1}{z^2} + \frac{2^2 - 1}{z^3} + \cdots.$$

Example 3

The function $z \longrightarrow \dfrac{1}{(1-z)(2-z)}$ of Example 2 can also be expanded about other points. Since it has a pole at 1 we can find a Laurent series about 1, in powers of $(z-1)$, convergent on the punctured disc $0 < |z-1| < 1$ (Fig. 16). See Problem 1(ii) of Section 8.6.

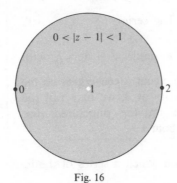

Fig. 16

We could evidently find a similar series expansion about the pole at 2.

Example 4

As our final example, we can find a series expansion of the function $z \longrightarrow \dfrac{1}{(1-z)(2-z)}$ about the point $\frac{3}{2}$, convergent on the disc $|z - \frac{3}{2}| < \frac{1}{2}$ (Fig. 17). The function is analytic on this disc, and so we get a Taylor series:

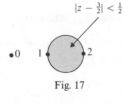

Fig. 17

$$\frac{1}{(1-z)(2-z)} = \frac{1}{1-z} - \frac{1}{2-z}$$

$$= \frac{1}{\frac{1}{2} + (z - \frac{3}{2})} - \frac{1}{\frac{1}{2} - (z - \frac{3}{2})}$$

$$= -2 \cdot \frac{1}{1 + 2(z - \frac{3}{2})} - 2 \cdot \frac{1}{1 - 2(z - \frac{3}{2})}$$

$$= -2(1 - 2(z - \tfrac{3}{2}) + 2^2(z - \tfrac{3}{2})^2 - \cdots)$$
$$\quad -2(1 + 2(z - \tfrac{3}{2}) + 2^2(z - \tfrac{3}{2})^2 + \cdots)$$

$$(\text{since } 2|z - \tfrac{3}{2}| < 1)$$

$$= -4(1 + 2^2(z - \tfrac{3}{2})^2 + \cdots).$$

We are now in a position to give a precise definition of the term "the Laurent series for a function". We have put off making this definition until now because we wished to emphasize, in the definition, the following very important point: a function may have several different Laurent series about the same point α (that is, in powers of $z - \alpha$) converging on different punctured discs or annular regions about α. For example, the function $z \longrightarrow \dfrac{1}{z(z-1)(z-2)(z-3)}$ is analytic on the following four regions.

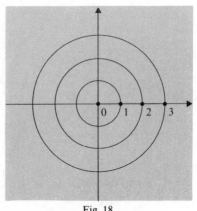

Fig. 18

 the punctured disc $0 < |z| < 1$;

 the annulus $1 < |z| < 2$;

 the annulus $2 < |z| < 3$;

 the "annulus" $|z| > 3$.

and has a different Laurent series about 0 for each of these regions (Fig. 18). Note also the use of the term "annulus" to describe the region $\{z : |z| > 3\}$, an alternative description of which is $\{z : 3 < |z| < \infty\}$.

So when we write about a Laurent series, we usually mention the region on which it converges. The only exception is that we shall sometimes use the phrase "the Laurent series for f about α" for the one which converges on the punctured disc $0 < |z - \alpha| < r$, when f has a singularity at α.

Definition

Suppose that the function f is analytic on the region $\{z : r_1 < |z - \alpha| < r_2\}$ (where $0 \leqslant r_1 < r_2$, and r_2 may be infinite). The series $\sum\limits_{n=-\infty}^{\infty} a_n(z - \alpha)^n$, where $a_n = \dfrac{1}{2\pi i} \displaystyle\int_C \dfrac{f(\zeta)}{(\zeta - \alpha)^{n+1}} d\zeta$, and C is a circle $|\zeta - \alpha| = \rho$ with $r_1 < \rho < r_2$, is called **the Laurent series for f about α convergent on the annulus** $r_1 < |z - \alpha| < r_2$. If f has a singularity at α, we may call the Laurent series for f about α convergent on the punctured disc $0 < |z - \alpha| < r_2$ just the **Laurent series for f about α**.

It is interesting to note that the set of points on which a series of the form $\sum\limits_{n=-\infty}^{\infty} a_n(z - \alpha)^n$ converges is either a punctured disc or an annulus (if it is not empty). The series of non-negative terms converges on a disc $|z - \alpha| < r_2$, for some r_2, while the series of negative terms converges for $\left| \dfrac{1}{z - \alpha} \right| < \dfrac{1}{r_1}$ for some r_1, that is, on $|z - \alpha| > r_1$. Thus the whole series converges on $r_1 < |z - \alpha| < r_2$ (provided $r_1 < r_2$).

Summary

We have seen that a Laurent series converges on a region of the form $r_1 < |z - \alpha| < r_2$ where $r_1 \geqslant 0$ and $r_2 > r_1$.

We have extended our results on Laurent series of Section 8.5 to cover the more general cases of an expansion about an essential singularity and an expansion on an annulus. The new feature that occurs is that the series may contain infinitely many negative powers of $(z - \alpha)$—in other words, its singular part may be a series. The Laurent series is still unique, and its coefficients are given by the same sort of formulas as we had in Section 8.5.

Self-Assessment Questions

1. What is the Laurent series for the function $z \longrightarrow \sin 1/z$ about its essential singularity at 0?

2. Find the Laurent series about 0 for the function $z \longrightarrow \dfrac{z}{(1 - z)(2 - z)}$ on the annulus $1 < |z| < 2$.

3. Briefly list the main steps in the proof of that part of Theorem 7 which establishes the existence of the Laurent series for a function about an essential singularity.

4. (i) How many different Laurent series about the point 1 does the function

   $$z \longrightarrow \frac{1}{z(z - 1)(z - 2)} \text{ have?}$$

   Where are these series convergent?

   (ii) Answer the same question for the same function, but for the point 2.

Solutions

1. $\dfrac{1}{z} - \dfrac{1}{3!} \cdot \dfrac{1}{z^3} + \dfrac{1}{5!} \cdot \dfrac{1}{z^5} - \cdots$.

2. $\cdots - \dfrac{1}{z^2} - \dfrac{1}{z} - 1 - \dfrac{1}{2}z - \dfrac{1}{2^2}z^2 - \dfrac{1}{2^3}z^3 - \cdots$.

3. Your answer should include at least the following points. To establish the existence of the Laurent series, we first use Cauchy's Formula for a punctured disc to write

   $$f(z) = \frac{1}{2\pi i} \int_{C_2} \frac{f(\zeta)}{\zeta - z} d\zeta - \frac{1}{2\pi i} \int_{C_1} \frac{f(\zeta)}{\zeta - z} d\zeta,$$

   where C_1, C_2 are circles centre α, radii ρ_1 and ρ_2 respectively, and $0 < \rho_1 < |z - \alpha| < \rho_2 < r$. We then use the formula

   $$\frac{1}{1 - \lambda} = \sum_{n=0}^{N} \lambda^n + \frac{\lambda^{N+1}}{1 - \lambda}$$

   first with $\lambda = \dfrac{z - \alpha}{\zeta - \alpha}$, then with $\lambda = \dfrac{\zeta - \alpha}{z - \alpha}$, to express the integrals as partial sums of the two parts of the Laurent series, with remainders. Finally we show that the remainder terms approach 0 as N gets large, by estimating the integrals in terms of which they are expressed. This shows that the two parts of the Laurent series converge to $\dfrac{1}{2\pi i} \int_{C_2} \dfrac{f(\zeta)}{\zeta - z} d\zeta$ and $-\dfrac{1}{2\pi i} \int_{C_1} \dfrac{f(\zeta)}{\zeta - z} d\zeta$,

   and that the series itself converges to $f(z)$.

4. (i) The function has

   a Laurent series about 1 convergent on the annulus $0 < |z - 1| < 1$,

   and

   a Laurent series about 1 convergent on the set $\{z : |z - 1| > 1\}$.

   (ii) The function has

   a Laurent series about 2 convergent on the annulus $0 < |z - 2| < 1$;

   a Laurent series about 2 convergent on the annulus $1 < |z - 2| < 2$;

   a Laurent series about 2 convergent on the set $\{z : |z - 2| > 2\}$.

8.8 USES OF LAURENT SERIES

The classification of singularities which we discussed in Section 8.1 may be simplified by the use of Laurent series about a singularity, which converge on a punctured disc. The part of such a series which consists of negative powers of $(z - \alpha)$ contains the relevant information. We call this the *singular part* of the function at α, as before.

Theorem 9

Suppose that f is analytic on the punctured disc $0 < |z - \alpha| < r$, and that its Laurent series about α is $\sum_{n=-\infty}^{\infty} a_n(z - \alpha)^n$. Then:

(i)   if $a_n = 0$ for all $n < 0$—in other words, if the singular part of the function is the zero function—then α is a removable singularity;

(ii) if $a_n = 0$ for all $n < -m$, $m > 0$, but $a_{-m} \neq 0$— in other words, if the singular part contains only finitely many terms—then α is a pole of order m;

(iii) if the singular part contains infinitely many terms, then α is an essential singularity.

Proof

(i)   In this case f is actually the sum of a convergent power series $\sum_{n=0}^{\infty} a_n(z - \alpha)^n$, and so has a removable singularity at α which is removed by setting $f(\alpha) = a_0$.

(ii) We can write $f(z) = \sum_{n=1}^{m} \dfrac{a_{-n}}{(z - \alpha)^n} + \phi(z)$, where ϕ is analytic on the disc $|z - \alpha| < r$. Thus $\lim_{z \to \alpha} (z - \alpha)^m f(z) = a_{-m} \neq 0$, and so α is a pole of order m.

(iii) A singularity which is neither removable nor a pole is an essential singularity. The Laurent series for a function about a removable singularity is in fact a Taylor series, so its singular part is the zero function; the singular part of the Laurent series of a function about a pole contains only finitely many terms, as we showed in Theorem 6. Thus if the function f has a singular part at α containing infinitely many terms, α must be an essential singularity of f. ∎

Warning: This theorem applies only to the Laurent series for a function about a singularity, convergent on a punctured disc; it does not apply to Laurent series convergent on an annulus. For example, in Self-Assessment Question 2 of Section 8.7, you showed that series

$$\cdots - \frac{1}{z^2} - \frac{1}{z} - 1 - \frac{1}{2}z - \frac{1}{2^2}z^2 - \frac{1}{2^3}z^3 - \cdots$$

is the Laurent series about 0 for $z \longrightarrow \dfrac{z}{(1 - z)(2 - z)}$, convergent on the annulus $1 < |z| < 2$. This series contains infinitely many negative powers of z, but it does not follow that the function has an essential singularity at 0.

Examples

1.   The Laurent series about 0 for the function $z \longrightarrow \sin 1/z$, $z \neq 0$, is

$$\frac{1}{z} - \frac{1}{3!}\cdot\frac{1}{z^3} + \frac{1}{5!}\cdot\frac{1}{z^5} - \cdots.$$

It contains infinitely many negative powers of z and converges on a "punctured disc", so 0 is an essential singularity.

2. Consider the function $z \longrightarrow \dfrac{z}{e^z - 1}$, $z \neq 0$. It has a singularity at 0. In order to find what kind of singularity we calculate the singular part of the function from its Laurent series about 0. Now $e^z = 1 + z + z^2 g(z)$, where g is entire. Thus $e^z - 1 = z(1 + zg(z))$, and

$$\frac{z}{e^z - 1} = \frac{z}{z(1 + zg(z))} = \frac{1}{1 + zg(z)}.$$

But this function is analytic on some disc centre 0 since $z \longrightarrow 1 + zg(z)$ is entire and has value 1 at $z = 0$. Thus the singular part of the function at 0 is the zero function, and the singularity is removable.

3. Knowledge of the type of a singularity may make it easier to calculate some coefficients of a Laurent series. For example, the function $z \longrightarrow \dfrac{1}{e^z - 1}$ has a simple pole at 0. This follows from Theorem 3 by showing that $\lim\limits_{z \to 0} \dfrac{z}{e^z - 1} = 1$, using l'Hôpital's Rule. Thus

$$\frac{1}{e^z - 1} = \frac{a_{-1}}{z} + a_0 + a_1 z + a_2 z^2 + \cdots$$

or equally

$$\left(\frac{a_{-1}}{z} + a_0 + a_1 z + a_2 z^2 + \cdots \right) \left(z + \frac{z^2}{2!} + \frac{z^3}{3!} + \cdots \right) = 1.$$

Multiplying up and comparing coefficients, we obtain the following equations for the coefficients a_{-1}, a_0, a_1 and a_2:

$$a_{-1} = 1,$$

$$a_0 + \frac{a_{-1}}{2!} = 0,$$

$$a_1 + \frac{a_0}{2!} + \frac{a_{-1}}{3!} = 0,$$

$$a_2 + \frac{a_1}{2!} + \frac{a_0}{3!} + \frac{a_{-1}}{4!} = 0.$$

The values of the coefficients may be calculated easily from these equations.

We have already pointed out that since the coefficients of a Laurent series are given by contour integrals, the calculation of certain integrals can be reduced to the calculation of coefficients of a Laurent series In particular, if the function f is analytic on the punctured disc $0 < |z - \alpha| < r$, and C is any circle centre α contained in the disc, then $\displaystyle\int_C f(\zeta)d\zeta = 2\pi i \cdot a_{-1}$ (where a_{-1} is the coefficient of $\dfrac{1}{(z - \alpha)}$ in the Laurent series of f about α). This method of integrating without integrating, and methods derived from it to cover more complicated situations, are very important, and will be dealt with fully in *Unit 10, The Calculus of Residues*. We shall end this unit with a few simple examples, to give you a taste of things to come.

The coefficient a_{-1} in the Laurent series is the one of principal interest from this point of view, and so has acquired a name of its own.

Definition

> If f has a singularity at α, the coefficient of $\dfrac{1}{(z - \alpha)}$ in its Laurent expansion about α is called the **residue of f at α** and is denoted by $\operatorname{Res}(f, \alpha)$.

So $\displaystyle\int_C f(\zeta)d\zeta$ is $2\pi i$ times the residue of f at α. The calculation of integrals around circles reduces to the calculation of residues, and in principle this can always be done if the Laurent series can be calculated. However, there are some cases which arise sufficiently often for it to be worthwhile to derive, and remember, a simple formula for the residue. We shall first give some examples of residues calculated from Laurent series directly, and then explain one of the short cuts.

Examples

4. The function $z \longrightarrow \dfrac{1}{z - \alpha}$ has a simple pole at α with residue 1—its Laurent series about α is just

$$\cdots + 0 \cdot \frac{1}{(z - \alpha)^2} + \frac{1}{z - \alpha} + 0 + 0 \cdot (z - \alpha) + \cdots.$$

Thus $\displaystyle\int_C \frac{1}{\zeta - \alpha}d\zeta = 2\pi i$, as always. On the other hand, the function $z \longrightarrow \dfrac{1}{(z - \alpha)^n}$, where $n \in \mathbf{N}$ and $n \geqslant 2$, although it has a singularity at α, has residue 0 there. Thus

$$\int_C \frac{1}{(\zeta - \alpha)^n}\,d\zeta = 0 \text{ if } n \geqslant 2.$$

5. The residue of $z \longrightarrow \sin 1/z$ at 0 is 1: see Example 1. Thus

$$\int_C \sin 1/\zeta\, d\zeta = 2\pi i.$$

Similarly, $\displaystyle\int_C \frac{1}{e^\zeta - 1}\, d\zeta = 2\pi i$: see Example 3.

6. The function $z \longrightarrow \dfrac{1}{(1 - z)(2 - z)}$ has simple poles at 1 and 2. Now

$$\frac{1}{(1 - z)(2 - z)} = \frac{1}{1 - z} - \frac{1}{2 - z} = -\frac{1}{z - 1} + \frac{1}{z - 2}$$

so the residue at 1 is -1, and the residue at 2 is 1. So, for example, if C is a circle centre 2 and of radius less than 1, then $\displaystyle\int_C \frac{1}{(1 - \zeta)(2 - \zeta)}d\zeta = -2\pi i.$

Notice that a function may have a singularity at a point, and yet have residue 0 there. Example 4 above is a case in point. It is a common error to suppose that if $\operatorname{Res}(f, \alpha) = 0$, or equally if $\displaystyle\int_C f = 0$ where C is some circle centre α, then f must be analytic on some disc containing α.

Simple poles probably constitute the class of singularity for which one most often has to calculate a residue. For example, a rational function p/q for which the polynomial q has a non-repeated factor $(z - \alpha)$, and for which $p(\alpha) \neq 0$, has a simple pole at α. We shall now derive a formula for the residue of such a rational function. To do this we use the following result, which we ask you to prove in Self-Assessment Question 2.

Result

If f has a simple pole at α, then

$$\text{Res}(f, \alpha) = \lim_{z \to \alpha} (z - \alpha) f(z).$$

The Cover-up Rule

If f is rational, and $f(z) = \dfrac{p(z)}{(z - \alpha)q(z)}$, where $p(\alpha) \neq 0$, $q(\alpha) \neq 0$, then by the above result,

$$\text{Res}(f, \alpha) = \lim_{z \to \alpha} (z - \alpha) f(z) = \frac{p(\alpha)}{q(\alpha)}.$$

This method of calculating the residue at a simple pole of a rational function is often called the "cover-up rule". What one does is simply cover up the factor $(z - \alpha)$ in the denominator which is responsible for the existence of the pole, and evaluate the remainder at α. It works only for simple poles.

Example

7.   If $f(z) = \dfrac{2}{z^2 + 1} = \dfrac{2}{(z - i)(z + i)}$, then we calculate $\text{Res}(f, i)$ as follows:

cover up the factor $z - i$, and evaluate the remainder at i, to get

$$\text{Res}(f, i) = \frac{2}{(z - i)(i + i)} = \frac{2}{2i} = -i.$$

Similarly, $\text{Res}(f, -i) = i$.

Summary

In this section we have collected together some results pertaining to the uses of Laurent series in classifying singularities and calculating integrals. In particular we have given some quick methods for calculating residues.

The only way of assessing whether you understand this material is to try some examples—and there are plenty in the next section. It's a no-holds-barred section: you may use any of the methods in this section, this unit, or indeed previous units. Part of the point of the exercise is to develop some skill in choosing the appropriate, and quickest, method.

Self-Assessment Questions

1.   For each of the following functions f, state what kind of singularity f has at the point α, and calculate $\text{Res}(f, \alpha)$.

(i) $f(z) = e^z/z$, $\alpha = 0$;

(ii) $f(z) = (e^z - 1)/z$, $\alpha = 0$;

(iii) $f(z) = 1/[z(z - 1)]$, $\alpha = 1$;

(iv) $f(z) = z^2 \cos 1/z$, $\alpha = 0$.

2.   Prove the Result above.

Solutions

1. (i) Simple pole; $\operatorname{Res}(f, \alpha) = 1$.

   (ii) Removable singularity; $\operatorname{Res}(f, \alpha) = 0$.

   (iii) Simple pole; $\operatorname{Res}(f, \alpha) = 1$.

   (iv) Essential singularity; $\operatorname{Res}(f, \alpha) = 0$.

2. If f has a simple pole at α, then

$$f(z) = \frac{a_{-1}}{z - \alpha} + a_0 + a_1(z - \alpha) + \cdots.$$

Multiply through by $(z - \alpha)$ and take the limit as z approaches α:

$$\lim_{z \to \alpha} (z - \alpha) f(z) = a_{-1} = \operatorname{Res}(f, \alpha).$$

8.9 PROBLEMS

You will find below a collection of integrals to evaluate. We have developed several methods of evaluating integrals so far in the course; apart from the method of residues outlined in the previous section, they are

(i)   direct calculation, using a parametrization of the contour—*Unit 4*;

(ii) the use of the Fundamental Theorem of Calculus (when the integrand is the derivative of a known function)—*Unit 4*;

(iii) the use of Cauchy's Theorem—*Unit 5*;

(iv) the use of Cauchy's Formulas, for integrals of the form $\int_\Gamma \frac{f(\zeta)}{(\zeta - \alpha)^n} d\zeta$—*Unit 5*;

(v)   integration by parts and by substitution—*Unit 5*.

In addition, the deformation lemma of *Unit 5* is often useful; and it is as well to remember that partial fractions can be used in calculating integrals of the form $\int_\Gamma \frac{f(\zeta)}{(\zeta - \alpha)(\zeta - \beta)} d\zeta$, for example.

Evaluate the following integrals, using the method you think most appropriate.

Try as many as you have time for.

1. $\int_C \operatorname{cosec} \zeta \, d\zeta$ where C is the circle $|\zeta| = 1$.

2. $\int_C \frac{\operatorname{cosec} \zeta}{\zeta} d\zeta$ where C is the circle $|\zeta| = 1$.

3. $\int_C \zeta \operatorname{cosec} \zeta \, d\zeta$ where C is the circle $|\zeta| = 1$.

4. $\int_C \frac{e^\zeta}{\zeta} d\zeta$ where C is the circle $|\zeta| = 1$.

5. $\int_C \frac{e^\zeta}{\zeta} d\zeta$ where C is the circle $|\zeta - 1| = \frac{1}{2}$.

6. $\int_C \frac{e^\zeta}{(\zeta - 1)^2} d\zeta$ where C is the circle $|\zeta - 1| = 1$.

7. $\int_C \sec^2 \zeta \, d\zeta$ where C is the circle $\left| \zeta - \frac{\pi}{2} \right| = 1$.

8. $\int_C \zeta \sec^2 \zeta \, d\zeta$ where C is the circle $\left| \zeta - \frac{\pi}{2} \right| = 1$.

9. $\int_C \frac{e^\zeta}{\zeta^2(\zeta - 1)} d\zeta$ where C is the circle $|\zeta| = \frac{1}{2}$.

10. $\int_C \frac{\zeta + \frac{1}{2} \sin 2\zeta}{(\zeta - \pi/4)^2} d\zeta$ where C is the circle $\left| \zeta - \frac{\pi}{4} \right| = 1$.

11. $\int_C \frac{\cosh \zeta}{\zeta^{n+1}} d\zeta$ where n is a positive integer and C is the circle $|\zeta| = 1$.

12. $\int_C \exp(1/\zeta^n) \, d\zeta$ where n is an integer and C is the circle $|\zeta| = 1$.

13. $\int_C \frac{\zeta e^{t\zeta}}{\zeta^2 + 1} d\zeta$ where t is a real number and C is the circle $|\zeta| = 2$.

14. $\displaystyle\int_C e^{1/\zeta} \sin 1/\zeta \, d\zeta$ where C is the circle $|\zeta| = 1$.

15. $\displaystyle\int_C \frac{1}{\zeta(1 - \cos \zeta)} d\zeta$ where C is the circle $|\zeta| = 1$.

16. $\displaystyle\int_C \frac{(\zeta - 1)^n}{\zeta(\zeta - 2)} d\zeta$ where n is an integer and C is the circle $|\zeta - 1| = \frac{1}{2}$.

17. $\displaystyle\int_C \frac{e^\zeta - 1}{\zeta(\zeta - 1)} d\zeta$ where C is the circle $|\zeta| = \frac{1}{2}$.

18. $\displaystyle\int_C \frac{\zeta - 2}{\zeta^3 - \zeta^2 + 4\zeta - 4} d\zeta$ where C is the circle $|\zeta - 1| = \frac{1}{2}$.

19. $\displaystyle\int_C \frac{e^\zeta - 1}{\sin^2 \zeta} d\zeta$ where C is the circle $|\zeta| = 1$.

20. $\displaystyle\int_C \frac{\cos \zeta}{4\zeta^2 - 4\pi\zeta + \pi^2} d\zeta$ where C is the circle $|\zeta| = \pi$.

Solutions

1. $2\pi i$. The function $z \longrightarrow \operatorname{cosec} z$ has a simple pole at 0 with residue 1.

2. 0. The function $z \longrightarrow \dfrac{\operatorname{cosec} z}{z}$ has a pole of order 2 at 0, but the residue is 0.

3. 0. The function $z \longrightarrow z \operatorname{cosec} z$ has a removable singularity at 0, so Cauchy's Theorem applies.

4. $2\pi i$. By Cauchy's Formula, or by observing that the residue of $z \longrightarrow \dfrac{e^z}{z}$ at 0 is 1.

5. 0. The integrand is analytic on a region containing the circle $|\zeta - 1| = \frac{1}{2}$ and its inside, so Cauchy's Theorem applies.

6. $2\pi ie$. By Cauchy's Formula for the first derivative, or by calculating the residue of $z \longrightarrow \dfrac{e^z}{(z - 1)^2}$ at the pole of order 2 at 1.

7. 0. By the Fundamental Theorem of Calculus ($\sec^2$ is the derivative of $\tan$), or by calculating the residue of $z \longrightarrow \sec^2 z$ at $\dfrac{\pi}{2}$, which is a pole of order 2.

8. $2\pi i$. Note that $\displaystyle\int_C \zeta \sec^2 \zeta \, d\zeta = \int_C \left(\zeta - \frac{\pi}{2}\right) \sec^2 \zeta \, d\zeta + \frac{\pi}{2} \int_C \sec^2 \zeta \, d\zeta$. The second integral is 0. The function $z \longrightarrow \left(z - \dfrac{\pi}{2}\right) \sec^2 z$ has a simple pole at $\dfrac{\pi}{2}$ with residue 1. Alternatively, $\displaystyle\int_C \zeta \sec^2 \zeta \, d\zeta = -\int_C \tan \zeta \, d\zeta$, by integration by parts; $\tan$ has a simple pole at $\dfrac{\pi}{2}$ with residue -1.

9. $-4\pi i$. The residue of the integrand at 0 is -2. (The singularity at 1 lies outside the contour.)

10. $2\pi i$. Cauchy's Formula for the first derivative gives the value of the integral as $2\pi i\left(1 + 2 \cdot \dfrac{1}{2} \cdot \cos\left(2 \cdot \dfrac{\pi}{4}\right)\right) = 2\pi i.$

11. $\frac{2\pi i}{n!}$ if n is even; 0 if n is odd. The residue at 0 is easily found from the Taylor series for cosh. Alternatively, use Cauchy's Formula for the nth derivative.

12. $2\pi i$ if $n = 1$; 0 otherwise. The Laurent series for the function $z \longrightarrow \exp(1/z^n)$ is $1 + \frac{1}{z^n} + \frac{1}{2!} \cdot \frac{1}{z^{2n}} + \cdots$.

13. $2\pi i \cos t$. Put $\frac{\zeta}{\zeta^2 + 1}$ into partial fractions and obtain

$$\int_c \frac{\zeta e^{t\zeta}}{\zeta^2 + 1} d\zeta = \tfrac{1}{2} \int_c \frac{e^{t\zeta}}{\zeta + i} d\zeta + \tfrac{1}{2} \int_c \frac{e^{t\zeta}}{\zeta - i} d\zeta.$$

Cauchy's Formula applies for each integral on the right-hand side, giving

$$\int_c \frac{e^{t\zeta}}{\zeta + i} d\zeta = 2\pi i \cdot e^{-it} \quad \text{and} \quad \int_c \frac{e^{t\zeta}}{\zeta - i} d\zeta = 2\pi i \cdot e^{it}.$$

14. $2\pi i$. The residue of the function at 0 (which is an essential singularity) is easily found to be 1, from multiplying the first few terms of the Laurent series about zero of $z \longrightarrow e^{1/z}$ and $z \longrightarrow \sin 1/z$.

15. $\frac{\pi i}{3}$. The residue of the function $z \longrightarrow \dfrac{1}{z(1 - \cos z)}$ at 0 (which is a pole of order 3) is calculated by finding the first few terms in the Laurent series, as follows:

$$\frac{1}{z(1 - \cos z)} = \frac{1}{z} \left(\frac{z^2}{2!} - \frac{z^4}{4!} + \cdots \right)^{-1}$$

$$= \frac{2}{z^3} \left(1 - \frac{z^2}{12} + \cdots \right)^{-1}$$

$$= \frac{2}{z^3} \left(1 + \frac{z^2}{12} + \cdots \right) = \frac{2}{z^3} + \frac{1}{6} \cdot \frac{1}{z} + \cdots;$$

so the residue is $\tfrac{1}{6}$.

16. $-2\pi i$ if n is odd and negative, 0 otherwise. The integral is $2\pi i$ times the coefficient of $(z - 1)^{-n-1}$ in the Laurent (actually Taylor) series for

$$z \longrightarrow \frac{1}{z(z - 2)} \text{ about 1. But}$$

$$\frac{1}{z(z - 2)} = \frac{1}{2} \left(\frac{1}{z - 2} - \frac{1}{z} \right)$$

$$= -\frac{1}{2} \left(\frac{1}{1 + (1 - z)} + \frac{1}{1 - (1 - z)} \right)$$

$$= -\tfrac{1}{2}([1 - (1 - z) + (1 - z)^2 - \cdots]$$

$$+ [1 + (1 - z) + (1 - z)^2 + \cdots])$$

$$= -1 - (1 - z)^2 - (1 - z)^4 - \cdots.$$

Thus the coefficient of $(z - 1)^{-n-1}$ is -1 if $-n - 1$ is non-negative and even, but zero otherwise.

17. 0. The integrand has a removable singularity at 0; the singularity at 1 lies outside the circle $|\zeta| = \tfrac{1}{2}$.

18. $-\dfrac{2\pi i}{5}$. The denominator of the integrand factorizes, so

$$\int_c \frac{\zeta - 2}{\zeta^3 - \zeta^2 + 4\zeta - 4} d\zeta = \int_c \frac{\zeta - 2}{(\zeta - 1)(\zeta^2 + 4)} d\zeta.$$

The residue at the relevant singularity—the simple pole at 1—is $-\tfrac{1}{5}$.

19. $2\pi i$. The integrand has a simple pole at 0. By the Result on page 52, the residue there is $\lim\limits_{z \to 0} \dfrac{z(e^z - 1)}{\sin^2 z} = 1$, by l'Hôpital's Rule.

20. $-\dfrac{\pi i}{2}$. The integrand is $z \longrightarrow \dfrac{\cos z}{4\left(z - \dfrac{\pi}{2}\right)^2}$, which has a simple pole at $\dfrac{\pi}{2}$.

The residue there, by the Result on page 51, is

$$\lim_{z \to \pi/2} \frac{\cos z}{4\left(z - \dfrac{\pi}{2}\right)} = \lim_{z \to \pi/2} \frac{-\sin z}{4} = -\frac{1}{4},$$

using l'Hôpital's Rule. Alternatively, Cauchy's Formula for the first derivative gives the same result in the same way.

Unit 9   Cauchy's Theorem II

Conventions

Before working through this text make sure you have read *A Guide to the Course: Complex Analysis*.

References to units of other Open University courses in mathematics take the form:

Unit M100 13, Integration II.

The set book for the course M231, Analysis, is M. Spivak, *Calculus*, paperback edition (W. A. Benjamin/Addison-Wesley, 1973). This is referred to as:

Spivak.

Optional Material

This course has been designed so that it is possible to make minor changes to the content in the light of experience. You should therefore consult the supplementary material to discover which sections of this text are not part of the course in the current academic year.

9.0 INTRODUCTION

There are two reasons why we return in this unit to a study of Cauchy's Theorem. The first is that there are various interesting consequences of Cauchy's Theorem for star regions that we did not have space to discuss in *Unit 5, Cauchy's Theorem I*, and *Unit 6, Taylor Series*: these lead to uniqueness results for analytic functions given certain "boundary conditions". The second, and more important, reason is that Cauchy's Theorem has so far been proved *only* for star regions: since this is a rather restrictive class of regions, we would like to prove a more general result. In this unit, we shall prove Cauchy's Theorem for a much wider class, in fact the widest possible class for which it can be proved—the simply-connected regions.

In the first reading section (9.1), we discuss further consequences of Cauchy's Theorem for star regions, in particular, the Maximum Principle and the Boundary Uniqueness Theorem. Next, in Section 9.3 we define the notion of simply-connected region and prove Cauchy's Theorem for simply-connected regions. In Section 9.5 we discuss various converses, consequences, and applications of Cauchy's Theorem, all of which are related by the topic of winding number.

The theoretical work in this unit culminates in the final reading section (9.7) with the Residue Theorem. Despite its theoretical antecedents, this is a very useful and practical result. However, there are no problems after this section, since you have to learn another technique, calculation of residues, before you can usefully apply the Residue Theorem. This technique, and many applications of the Residue Theorem, will be discussed in *Unit 10, The Calculus of Residues*.

Television

In the sixth television programme associated with the course we look at the structure of two proofs from this unit: the proofs of the Local Maximum Principle, and of Cauchy's Theorem for simply-connected regions.

9.1 THE MAXIMUM PRINCIPLE

Do you remember Cauchy's Formula? It says that if C is a circle and f is a function analytic on some region containing C and its inside (which we shall denote by R) then f is uniquely determined in the region R by its values *on* C, by means of the formula:

$$f(z) = \frac{1}{2\pi i} \int_C \frac{f(\zeta)}{\zeta - z} \, d\zeta, \quad z \in R.$$

It is possible to strengthen this result a bit. Note that the closure $\bar{R}$ of R is just $R \cup C$. We need suppose only that f is analytic on R and continuous on $\bar{R}$ for the above formula to apply. (This is proved by slightly shrinking the circle C and applying uniform continuity of f—see Problem 6 of Section 5.8 of *Unit 5*.)

Thus at least for an open disc R, a function analytic on R and continuous on $\bar{R}$ is uniquely determined by its values on the *boundary* of R. To put it another way: if both f and g are analytic on R and continuous on $\bar{R}$, and $f(\zeta) = g(\zeta)$ for all ζ on the boundary of R, then $f = g$ on R.

Our main aim in this section is to generalize this result to *all* bounded regions R. As you might expect, we lose something: we no longer get a formula expressing $f(z)$ for points z in R in terms of the values of f on the boundary of R. However, this generalization of the result is important for theoretical work, and we shall show in Section 9.5 that in special cases a formula *can* be derived.

You have already seen some uniqueness theorems—for example, Theorem 16 of *Unit 6*, which states that if R is a region and S a subset of R with a cluster point in R, then a function f analytic on R is uniquely determined by its values on S. This theorem followed from Corollary 2 to Theorem 15 in *Unit 6*, which states that a function analytic on a region is rather limited in its behaviour, in that its zeros are isolated. We shall adopt an analogous approach, and first prove the following "limitation theorem" on local maxima.

Theorem 1 (The Local Maximum Principle)

Let f be analytic on a region R. If f is *not* constant on R, then $|f|$ has *no* local maximum at any point in R.

There are some items of terminology that we should explain. We say that a real-valued function ϕ has a **maximum on** a set S at a point $a \in S$ if $\phi(a)$ is the maximum of ϕ on S, that is if $\phi(a) \geq \phi(z)$ for all $z \in S$. Then we say that ϕ has a **local maximum on** S at $a \in S$ if there is some neighbourhood D of a such that ϕ has a maximum on $D \cap S$ at a. If S is open, we can choose D to lie in S: then we drop the phrase "on S". The definitions of **minimum** and **local minimum** are left for you to supply (see Self-Assessment Question 1). As expected, we say that f is *constant on* a set S if there is some constant a such that $f(z) = a$ for all $z \in S$.

The proof of Theorem 1 uses a result from real analysis which we shall state as a lemma.

Lemma

Let g be a real function continuous on the interval $[a, b]$ and such that $g \geq 0$ on $[a, b]$. If $\int_a^b g = 0$ then $g = 0$ on $[a, b]$.

Proof

We certainly have $\int_a^b g \geq 0$ (since $g \geq 0$). We now argue by contradiction. Suppose that $g(t_0) > 0$ for some $t_0 \in [a, b]$. Assume first that $a < t_0 < b$. Then there is some $\delta > 0$ such that if $t_0 - \delta \leq t \leq t_0 + \delta$ then $g(t) > \frac{1}{2}g(t_0)$: see Fig. 1.

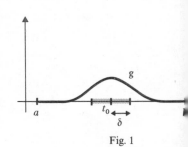

Fig. 1

Hence

$$\int_a^b g = \int_a^{t_0-\delta} g + \int_{t_0-\delta}^{t_0+\delta} g + \int_{t_0+\delta}^b g$$

$$\geqslant 0 + 2\delta \cdot \tfrac{1}{2}g(t_0) + 0$$

$$= \delta g(t_0) > 0.$$

Clearly this argument works only for $t_0 \in (a, b)$: we leave it to you to modify it appropriately for $t_0 = a$ or $t_0 = b$: see Self-Assessment Question 2. Thus, in either case, $\int_a^b g > 0$, which contradicts the hypothesis that $\int_a^b g = 0$. ■

Proof of Theorem 1

We argue by contradiction. Suppose that f is not constant on R, but that $|f|$ has a local maximum at a point α in R. Thus, since R is open, there is $\varepsilon > 0$ such that

$$|f(z)| \leqslant |f(\alpha)| \quad \text{whenever } |z - \alpha| < \varepsilon. \tag{*}$$

We now apply a consequence of Cauchy's Formula, Gauss's Mean Value Theorem—see Problem 4 of Section 5.6 of *Unit 5*—and also the estimation result $\left|\int_a^b \phi\right| \leqslant \int_a^b |\phi|$—see Problem 7 of Section 4.2 of *Unit 4, Integration*. From Gauss's Mean Value Theorem

$$f(\alpha) = \frac{1}{2\pi} \int_0^{2\pi} f(\alpha + re^{i\theta})\, d\theta;$$

therefore

$$|f(\alpha)| = \frac{1}{2\pi}\left|\int_0^{2\pi} f(\alpha + re^{i\theta})\, d\theta\right|$$

$$\leqslant \frac{1}{2\pi}\int_0^{2\pi} |f(\alpha + re^{i\theta})|\, d\theta, \quad \text{using the result that } \left|\int_a^b \phi\right| \leqslant \int_a^b |\phi|,$$

$$\leqslant \frac{1}{2\pi}\int_0^{2\pi} |f(\alpha)|\, d\theta, \quad \text{since } |f(\alpha + re^{i\theta})| \leqslant |f(\alpha)| \text{ by } (*),$$

$$= |f(\alpha)|,$$

and so $|f(\alpha)| = \dfrac{1}{2\pi}\displaystyle\int_0^{2\pi} |f(\alpha + re^{i\theta})|\, d\theta$, that is,

$$\int_0^{2\pi} (|f(\alpha)| - |f(\alpha + re^{i\theta})|)\, d\theta = 0.$$

Applying the lemma to the real continuous non-negative function

$$g(\theta) = |f(\alpha)| - |f(\alpha + re^{i\theta})|,$$

it follows that $g(\theta) = 0$, that is

$$|f(\alpha)| = |f(\alpha + re^{i\theta})|, \quad \text{whenever } 0 \leqslant \theta \leqslant 2\pi.$$

Because this holds for any $r \in (0, \varepsilon)$, $|f(\alpha)| = |f(z)|$ whenever $0 < |z - \alpha| < \varepsilon$, that is, $|f|$ is constant on $D = \{z : |z - \alpha| < \varepsilon\}$. Hence by Theorem 17 of *Unit 3, Differentiation*, f is constant on D, and so, by Theorem 16 of *Unit 6*, f is constant on the whole region R. This is a contradiction. ■

Let us look at the geometrical significance of Theorem 1. Suppose, for simplicity, that f is non-constant and entire, and consider the graph of $|f|$, which may be thought of as the graph of $F:(x, y) \longrightarrow F(x, y)$, where $F(x, y) = |f(x + iy)|$. (In other words the graph of $|f|$ is a surface in three dimensions.) Then it cannot look like that in Fig. 2, in a neighbourhood of any point.

Fig. 2

Note also, that by Liouville's Theorem, $|f|$ is unbounded and since the image of C under $|f|$ is an interval, $|f|$ takes all sufficiently large real values.

There is a corollary of Theorem 1, which is very often the form in which it is actually applied. To prove it we require an easy "uniqueness lemma', which is also useful on other occasions.

Lemma

Let S be a set, and f, g be functions continuous on $\bar{S}$, such that $f = g$ on S. Then $f = g$ on $\bar{S}$.

Proof

Let $h = f - g$; then $h = 0$ on S. We have to prove that $h = 0$ on $\bar{S}$. So suppose that for some $a \in \bar{S} - S$, $h(a) \neq 0$. Then there is some $\delta > 0$ such that if $z \in S$ and $|z - a| < \delta$, then $h(z) \neq 0$. Since a is a cluster point of S, there is $z_0 \in S$ such that $0 < |z_0 - a| < \delta$, and so $h(z_0) \neq 0$; but $h(z_0) = 0$ since $z_0 \in S$. This is a contradiction, and so $h(a) = 0$. ∎

Now we can state and prove the Corollary to Theorem 1.

Corollary (The Maximum Principle)

Let f be analytic on a bounded region R, and continuous on $\bar{R}$. Then $|f|$ has a maximum on $\bar{R}$ at a point on the boundary of R.

Proof

Since R is bounded, it is contained in some closed disc, and so $\bar{R}$ is bounded. By the Corollary to Theorem 12 in *Unit 2*, $|f|$ has a maximum on $\bar{R}$ at some point $a \in \bar{R}$ (since $|f|$ is continuous on $\bar{R}$, and $\bar{R}$ is closed and bounded). If $a \notin R$ then the proof is complete; so suppose that $a \in R$. By Theorem 1, f is constant on R, that is, there is some k such that $f(z) = k$, $z \in R$. But by the lemma, $f(z) = k$ for all $z \in \bar{R}$. Hence f is constant on $\bar{R}$ and so $|f|$ has a maximum at *every* point of the boundary of R. ∎

It is now very easy to deduce from this corollary the uniqueness theorem we were aiming for.

Theorem 2   (The Boundary Uniqueness Theorem)

Let f and g be analytic on a bounded region R and continuous on $\bar{R}$. Suppose that $f = g$ on the boundary of R. Then $f = g$ on R.

Proof

We look at the difference $f - g$. Since $f - g$ is analytic on R and continuous on $\bar{R}$, $|f - g|$ attains its maximum on $\bar{R}$ at the boundary of R. Since $f = g$ on the boundary, this maximum value is 0. Hence $|f(z) - g(z)| \leqslant 0$ for all $z \in R$, that is, $f = g$ on R. ∎

The problems after this section will discuss refinements of this uniqueness theorem, and other ways of using the Maximum Principle to discover limitations on the behaviour of analytic functions. But we shall give one application here, which, although it can be done by more elementary methods, is nevertheless instructive.

Example

Let S be the closed square $\{z : 0 \leqslant \mathrm{Re}\, z \leqslant \pi$ and $0 \leqslant \mathrm{Im}\, z \leqslant \pi\}$. Find the maximum value of $|\sin z|$ for $z \in S$.

Solution

Let $f(z) = \sin z$. By the Maximum Principle, $|f|$ attains its maximum on S at the boundary of S. So we must look at the four sides of the square (Fig. 3).

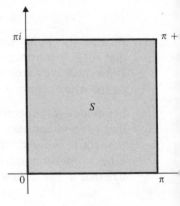

Fig. 3

(i)   Side $[0, \pi]$

If $0 \leqslant x \leqslant \pi$, $|\sin x| \leqslant 1$, and $\left|\sin \dfrac{\pi}{2}\right| = \sin \dfrac{\pi}{2} = 1$.

(ii)   Side $[0, \pi i]$

If $0 \leqslant y \leqslant \pi$, $|\sin iy| = \sinh y \leqslant \sinh \pi$ (with equality at $y = \pi$).

In order to deal with the other two sides we require the following result.

If $z = x + iy$, then

$$\sin z = \sin x \cosh y + i \cos x \sinh y,$$

and so

$$
\begin{aligned}
|\sin z|^2 &= \sin^2 x \cosh^2 y + \cos^2 x \sinh^2 y \\
&= \sin^2 x + \sin^2 x \sinh^2 y + \cos^2 x \sinh^2 y \\
&= \sin^2 x + \sinh^2 y. \qquad\qquad (*)
\end{aligned}
$$

(iii)   Side $[\pi, \pi + \pi i]$

If $x = \pi$ and $0 \leqslant y \leqslant \pi$, then from $(*)$

$$
\begin{aligned}
|\sin z|^2 &= \sinh^2 y \\
&\leqslant \sinh^2 \pi \quad \text{(with equality at } y = \pi),
\end{aligned}
$$

and so $|\sin z| \leqslant \sinh \pi$.

(iv)   Side $[\pi i, \pi + \pi i]$

If $y = \pi$ and $0 \leqslant x \leqslant \pi$, then from $(*)$

$$
\begin{aligned}
|\sin z|^2 &= \sin^2 x + \sinh^2 \pi \\
&\leqslant 1 + \sinh^2 \pi \quad \left(\text{with equality at } x = \frac{\pi}{2}\right) \\
&= \cosh^2 \pi,
\end{aligned}
$$

and so $|\sin z| \leqslant \cosh \pi$.

Since $\cosh \pi \geqslant \sinh \pi \geqslant 1$, the maximum of $|f|$ on S is $\cosh \pi$, and occurs at the point $\dfrac{\pi}{2} + \pi i$.

Summary

In this section we have proved the Local Maximum Principle and its corollary, the Maximum Principle; the proof used Gauss's Mean Value Theorem, estimation of an integral, and a result on integrals from real analysis. We then proved an important application of the Maximum Principle called the Boundary Uniqueness Theorem, which tells us that, loosely speaking, an analytic function is determined by its boundary values.

Self-Assessment Questions

1.   Give definitions of the following (where ϕ is a real-valued function of a complex variable):

(a) ϕ has a minimum on S at a,

(b) ϕ has a local minimum on S at a.

2.   Show that if g is a real function, continuous and non-negative on $[a, b]$, and $g(a) > 0$, then $\displaystyle\int_a^b g > 0$.

3.　Summarize in words the statements of

(a)　the Local Maximum Principle,

(b)　the Boundary Uniqueness Theorem.

4.　Let f be analytic on the open disc $\{z:|z| < 1\}$ and continuous on the closed disc $\{z:|z| \leqslant 1\}$. What can you say about the set S of points at which $|f|$ has a maximum?

5.　Let f be analytic and non-constant on the bounded region R, and continuous on $\bar{R}$. Let $M = \max\{|f(z)|:z \in \bar{R} - R\}$.

Show that $M > |f(z)|$ for all $z \in R$.

6.　Let f be entire. Define the real function M by $M(r) = \max\{|f(z)|:|z| = r\}$. Show that $M:[0, \infty) \longrightarrow \mathbf{R}$ is a *non-decreasing function*, that is,

$$M(r) \leqslant M(s) \text{ if } r \leqslant s.$$

7.　Let $\phi(x, y) = \exp(-(x^2 + y^2))$. Why is ϕ not of the form $|f|$ for any entire function f?

Solutions

1.　(a)　ϕ has a minimum on S at a if $\phi(a) \leqslant \phi(z)$ for all $z \in S$.

(b)　ϕ has a local minimum on S at a if there is some neighbourhood D of a such that ϕ has a minimum on $D \cap S$ at a.

2.　There is a $\delta > 0$ such that $g(t) > \frac{1}{2}g(a)$ if $a \leqslant t \leqslant a + \delta$, and so

$$\int_a^b g = \int_a^{a+\delta} g + \int_{a+\delta}^b g \geqslant \delta \cdot \tfrac{1}{2}g(a) + 0 > 0.$$

3.　(a)　No function analytic on a bounded region can have a local maximum of its modulus in that region, unless it is constant.

(b)　Any function analytic on a region and continuous on the closure is uniquely determined by its values on the boundary.

4.　If f is constant on $\{z:|z| < 1\}$, every point of $\{z:|z| \leqslant 1\}$ belongs to S. Otherwise, S is contained in the circle $\{z:|z| = 1\}$.

5.　By the Maximum Principle, $M \geqslant |f(z)|$ for all $z \in R$. It remains to show that $M \neq |f(z)|$ for all $z \in R$. If $M = |f(\alpha)|$ for some $\alpha \in R$, then $|f|$ has a maximum at α, which contradicts the Local Maximum Principle.

6.　If $r < s$ then $\{z:|z| = r\} \subseteq \{z:|z| < s\}$, and so $|f(z)| \leqslant M(s)$ whenever $|z| = r$, by the Maximum Principle. Hence $M(r) \leqslant M(s)$.

7.　If $\phi = |f|$, where f is entire, then $|f|$ is non-constant and has a maximum at 0, which contradicts the Local Maximum Principle. (It also contradicts Liouville's Theorem.)

9.2 PROBLEMS

1. Let D be the disc $\{z:|z| \leqslant 1\}$. Find the maximum value of $z \longrightarrow |\exp(z^2)|$ on D, and where it occurs.

2. (a) Prove the **Minimum Principle**, which can be stated as follows. If f is analytic on a bounded region R, and continuous and non-zero on $\bar{R}$, then $|f|$ attains its minimum on $\bar{R}$ at the boundary of R.

   (Hint: Apply the Maximum Principle to a suitable function.)

   (b) Find the minimum of $z \longrightarrow |\exp(z^2)|$ on the disc $D = \{z:|z| \leqslant 1\}$.

There is another global result on the behaviour of analytic functions that should come to mind. This is Liouville's Theorem (Theorem 10 of *Unit 5*): If f is entire and bounded, then f is constant. In addition, in Problem 2 of Section 5.8 of *Unit 5*, we showed that the conclusion of Liouville's Theorem still held if "f is bounded" was weakened to "Re f is bounded"—the result was proved by applying Liouville's Theorem to e^f. A similar trick enables us to strengthen the Maximum Principle.

---

3. (a) Show that if f is analytic on a region R and f is not constant then Re f has no local maximum on R.

   (b) Deduce the same for "local minimum".

4. Let $f(z) = \exp(z^2)$. Find the maximum of Re f on the closed disc $\{z:|z| \leqslant 1\}$, and one point where it occurs.

5. Just as the Maximum Principle was used to prove a uniqueness theorem, so Problem 3 can be used to establish an analogous result.

   Let f and g be analytic on the bounded region R, and continuous on $\bar{R}$. Suppose that Re $f =$ Re g on the boundary of R. Show that there is $c \in \mathbf{R}$ such that

   $$f(z) - g(z) = ic \quad \text{for all } z \in R.$$

6. The Maximum Principle is a corollary to Theorem 1, the proof of which uses Theorem 17 of *Unit 3*, which depends on partial derivatives. As we said in the Introduction to *Unit 3*, it is possible to give complex analytic proofs of the crucial results which we obtain by means of partial derivatives. The following problem shows how a knowledge of partial derivatives may be avoided in the proof of the Maximum Principle.

   If you are not familiar with partial derivatives you should try this problem; if you are familiar with partial derivatives, you will still find this problem of value for revision, so do not omit it unless you are short of time.

   Let f be analytic on a region R. Suppose that $|f|$ has a local maximum at a point $\alpha \in R$, and that $f(\alpha) \neq 0$. By considering the functions $\theta \longrightarrow \text{Re} \dfrac{f(\alpha + re^{i\theta})}{f(\alpha)}$ for suitable r, prove that f is constant on R.

Solutions

1. By the Maximum Principle, the maximum occurs on the boundary of D, that is, the circle $|z| = 1$. If $z = e^{i\theta}$, then
$$\exp(z^2) = \exp(e^{i\theta})^2 = \exp(e^{2i\theta})$$
$$= \exp(\cos 2\theta + i \sin 2\theta),$$
and so
$$|\exp(z^2)| = |e^{\cos 2\theta}| \cdot |e^{i \sin 2\theta}| = e^{\cos 2\theta}.$$
Now $e^{\cos 2\theta} \leqslant e$ (with equality for $\theta = 0$ and $\theta = \pi$).
Hence the maximum value of $z \longrightarrow |\exp(z^2)|$ on D is e, and it occurs at the points e^0 and $e^{\pi i}$, that is, 1 and -1.

2. (a) The function $1/f$ is analytic on R and continuous on $\bar{R}$. Hence by the Maximum Principle, there is a point α on the boundary of R such that for all $z \in \bar{R}$,

$$|1/f|(\alpha) \geq |1/f|(z),$$

that is, $1/|f(\alpha)| \geq 1/|f(z)|$, and so

$$|f(\alpha)| \leq |f(z)|.$$

Hence $|f|$ attains its minimum on $\bar{R}$ at α.

(b) By part (a), the minimum occurs at $z = e^{i\theta}$ for some θ. Now

$$|\exp(z^2)| = e^{\cos 2\theta} \geq e^{-1}.$$

Thus the minimum is e^{-1}, and it occurs at the points $i = e^{i\pi/2}$ and $-i = e^{-i\pi/2}$.

3. (a) Since exp is entire, e^f is analytic on R. Also e^f is not constant, because f is not constant—see Problem 2 of Section 5.8 of *Unit 5*. Thus $|e^f|$ has no local maximum at a point in R. Suppose that Re f has a local maximum at $\alpha \in R$, that is, for some $\varepsilon > 0$,

$$\operatorname{Re} f(\alpha) \geq \operatorname{Re} f(z) \quad \text{if } |z - \alpha| < \varepsilon.$$

Then

$$|e^{f(\alpha)}| = |e^{\operatorname{Re} f(\alpha)}| \cdot |e^{i \operatorname{Im} f(\alpha)}|$$

$$= e^{\operatorname{Re} f(\alpha)}$$

$$\geq e^{\operatorname{Re} f(z)}$$

$$= |e^{f(z)}| \quad \text{if } |z - \alpha| < \varepsilon,$$

since $\exp : \mathbf{R} \longrightarrow \mathbf{R}$ is increasing. Thus $|e^f|$ has a local maximum at α. This is a contradiction, and so Re f has no local maximum on R.

(b) The function e^f is analytic and non-zero on R. Hence by the method of Problem 2, $|e^f|$ has no local minimum in R. Thus by the method of part (a), Re f has no local minimum.

4. Let $\phi = \operatorname{Re} f$. Since

$$e^{(x+iy)^2} = e^{x^2-y^2} e^{2ixy},$$

$$\phi(x, y) = e^{x^2-y^2} \cos 2xy.$$

By Problem 3, the maximum of ϕ on D occurs at $(x, y) = (\cos \theta, \sin \theta)$ for some θ (that is, on the boundary of D).

Now

$$\phi(\cos \theta, \sin \theta) = e^{\cos^2\theta - \sin^2\theta} \cos(2 \cos \theta \sin \theta)$$

$$= e^{\cos 2\theta} \cos(\sin 2\theta).$$

We can now find the maximum of the real function

$$h(\theta) = \phi(\cos \theta, \sin \theta)$$

by calculus methods. By differentiating,

$$h'(\theta) = e^{\cos 2\theta}[- \sin(\sin 2\theta) \cdot 2 \cos 2\theta - 2 \sin 2\theta \cdot \cos(\sin 2\theta)],$$

and so $h'(0) = 0$. To prove that h has a maximum at 0, we need not differentiate again or examine the sign of $h'(\theta)$: we need only apply the definition of maximum.

Now $h(0) = e^{\cos 0} \cos 0 = e$; also $e \geq e^{\cos 2\theta}$ and $1 \geq \cos(\sin 2\theta)$ for any θ.

Thus $h(\theta) \leq h(0) = e$, and so h has a maximum at 0. Hence ϕ has a maximum at the point 1, and the maximum value of ϕ is e.

5. Let $h = f - g$. Then h is analytic on R and continuous on $\bar{R}$: thus Re h is continuous on $\bar{R}$. Hence Re h attains both a maximum and a minimum on $\bar{R}$. By the method of the corollary to Theorem 1 applied to the results of Problem 3, these are attained on the boundary. But Re $h = 0$ on the boundary, and so Re $h = 0$ on R. Thus Im h is analytic on R (because $h = i \operatorname{Im} h$) and so has constant value c, say (by Theorem 17 of *Unit 3*).

Hence

$$f(z) - g(z) = h(z) = i \operatorname{Im} h(z) = ic \quad \text{for all } z \in R.$$

6. Since $|f|$ has a local maximum at α, there is $\varepsilon > 0$ such that

$$|f(z)| \leqslant |f(\alpha)| \quad \text{whenever } |z - \alpha| < \varepsilon. \qquad (*)$$

Let $0 < r < \varepsilon$; then

$$f(\alpha) = \frac{1}{2\pi} \int_0^{2\pi} f(\alpha + re^{i\theta})\, d\theta$$

and so

$$1 = \frac{1}{2\pi} \int_0^{2\pi} \frac{f(\alpha + re^{i\theta})}{f(\alpha)}\, d\theta \qquad (\dagger)$$

Let $g_r(\theta) = \operatorname{Re} \dfrac{f(\alpha + re^{i\theta})}{f(\alpha)}$. Then

$$g_r(\theta) \leqslant \left| \frac{f(\alpha + re^{i\theta})}{f(\alpha)} \right| \leqslant 1, \quad \text{by } (*),$$

and

$$1 = \frac{1}{2\pi} \int_0^{2\pi} g_r(\theta)\, d\theta, \quad \text{by } (\dagger).$$

Hence by the lemma on page 60, $g_r(\theta) = 1$ if $0 \leqslant \theta \leqslant 2\pi$; in other words,

$$\operatorname{Re} \frac{f(\alpha + re^{i\theta})}{f(\alpha)} = 1,$$

and so

$$\operatorname{Im} \frac{f(\alpha + re^{i\theta})}{f(\alpha)} = 0$$

(since if $|w| \leqslant 1$ and $\operatorname{Re} w = 1$ then $\operatorname{Im} w = 0$).

Thus $\dfrac{f(\alpha + re^{i\theta})}{f(\alpha)} = 1$, for all $\theta \in [0, 2\pi]$, and $r \in (0, \varepsilon)$.

Hence f is constant on a neighbourhood of α, and so in R, by Theorem 16 of *Unit 6*.

(Note that if $f(\alpha) = 0$, the conclusion follows immediately. With this observation, the above solution becomes a proof of the Maximum Principle. Note that Theorem 17 of *Unit 3* can be deduced as a corollary.)

9.3 SIMPLY-CONNECTED REGIONS AND CAUCHY'S THEOREM

Let us go back to the original motivation for the uniqueness theorem proved in Section 9.1, which was Cauchy's Formula. As often happens when generalizing theorems, we have generalized one aspect (uniqueness) of Cauchy's Formula but seem to have abandoned the other (the formula). The formula part says that in a region R, which is the inside of a circle, the values of an analytic function at points in R are given by a formula in terms of the values on the circle. Can we replace the circle by other simple-closed contours and still get such a formula? The answer is yes, but this fact cannot be proved by the simple-minded geometric method of *Unit 5*. We have to use more powerful techniques, in particular a more general version of Cauchy's Theorem.

Do you recall the procedure we adopted in *Unit 2* to find an analogue of the Intermediate Value Theorem? We defined a set to be *connected* if the Intermediate Value Theorem (in slightly disguised form) held for it, worked towards a more practical version, *polygonally-connected*, and ended by proving the equivalence of these two notions. In this section and the next reading section we shall follow a similar procedure to investigate Cauchy's Theorem. To begin with, we make the following key definition.

Definition

> A region R is said to be a **Cauchy region** if whenever Γ is a closed contour in R and f is a function analytic on R then
>
> $$\int_\Gamma f = 0.$$

(In other words, R is a Cauchy region if Cauchy's Theorem holds in R.) Then we can state our task as follows:

Task

Find a useful characterization of Cauchy regions.

If we can do this, we can generalize Cauchy's Theorem to this new class of regions.

From Cauchy's Theorem in *Unit 5*, we know that any star region is a Cauchy region. But it may have occurred to you when reading the proof of Cauchy's Formula in *Unit 5*, that there are regions to which Cauchy's Theorem applies and which are not star regions, and that they could be obtained by "glueing together" star regions in an appropriate way.

Suppose R is the open *semi-annulus* shown in Fig. 4 with outer and inner radii r_1 and r. Now R is not a star region, but we are going to express it as the union of two overlapping star regions, under certain conditions.

Consider the *annular sector* of R of angle θ, shown in Fig. 5. This will be a star region provided the tangents to the inner circle meet at a point F *inside* the sector: then any point in the darker shaded region will in fact be a star. By elementary trigonometry, F lies inside the sector provided that $OF < r_1$, that is

$$r \sec \frac{\theta}{2} < r_1, \text{ or } \cos \frac{\theta}{2} < \frac{r}{r_1}, \text{ so that } \theta < 2 \arccos \frac{r}{r_1}. \text{ Now assume that } \frac{r}{r_1} < \frac{1}{\sqrt{2}},$$

then $\arccos \dfrac{r}{r_1} > \dfrac{\pi}{4}$, and so $2 \arccos \dfrac{r}{r_1} > \dfrac{\pi}{2}$. Choose θ such that

$$\frac{\pi}{2} < \theta < 2 \arccos \frac{r}{r_1},$$

and let A and B be the annular sectors of angle θ shown in Fig. 6: then A and B are star regions and $R = A \cup B$.

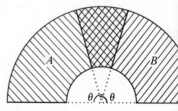

Fig. 4

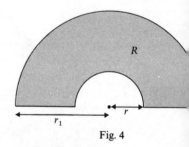

Fig. 5

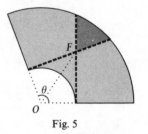

Fig. 6

Now let Γ be the closed contour in R shown in Fig. 7 and f be a function analytic on R. If we bisect R along its axis of symmetry we can split Γ into contours Γ_1 and Γ_2 such that

$$\int_\Gamma f = \int_{\Gamma_1} f + \int_{\Gamma_2} f,$$

since the integrals along the straight line PQ cancel (Fig. 8). Now Γ_1 lies in A and Γ_2 lies in B, so that $\int_{\Gamma_1} f = \int_{\Gamma_2} f = 0$, by Cauchy's Theorem for the star regions A and B respectively. Hence $\int_\Gamma f = 0$.

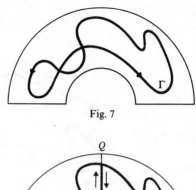

Fig. 7

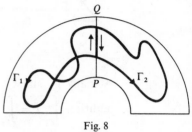

Fig. 8

This *seems* to establish that R is a Cauchy region. There is one small snag, though. An arbitrary contour Γ might cross the line PQ infinitely often, and it might be impossible to see how to decompose Γ into Γ_1 and Γ_2—and even if one could decompose Γ into paths Γ_1 and Γ_2 they might not be *contours*. However, we can get round this snag as follows. Just as to prove connectedness we did not consider *all* arcs, so it is unlikely that to prove a region is a Cauchy region we shall, in the end, have to consider all closed contours. There *is* a natural class of contours for which the decomposition above will work—the polygonal contours.

Recall from *Unit 2* that a polygonal line is a union $L = [z_1, z_2] \cup \cdots \cup [z_{n-1}, z_n]$ of line segments—equivalently, in the notation of *Unit 4*, $L = [z_1, z_2] + \cdots + [z_{n-1}, z_n]$ is a contour. Thus we shall often call a polygonal line a *polygonal contour*. A closed polygonal contour is called a *polygon*; a simple-closed polygon is called a *simple polygon*. Fig. 9 shows these three kinds of contour: note that a point labelled with an integer n represents the point z_n.

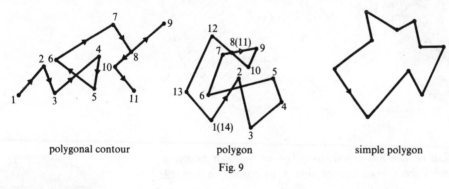

| polygonal contour | polygon | simple polygon |

Fig. 9

Given a polygonal contour $L = [z_1, z_2] + \cdots + [z_{n-1}, z_n]$, the points $z_1, \ldots, z_n$ are called *vertices* of L and the line segments $[z_1, z_2], \ldots, [z_{n-1}, z_n]$ are called *edges* of L. Note that the intersection of two edges is not necessarily a vertex. (See Fig. 9.)

In order to use polygons, we introduce a modification of our notion of Cauchy region. We shall call a region R **polygonally-Cauchy** if $\int_\Gamma f = 0$ whenever Γ is a polygon in R and f is analytic on R. Clearly a Cauchy region is polygonally-Cauchy: we shall prove the converse later. But at least now we can fix up our previous example. Since any line meets a polygon in a finite number (possibly zero) of points or lines it is easy to see how to decompose a polygon Γ into polygons Γ_1 and Γ_2 by splitting it with the line PQ.

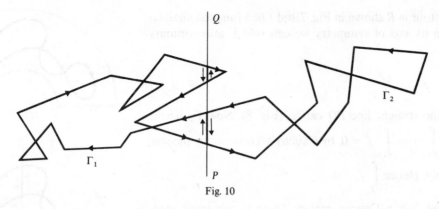

Fig. 10

Actually Γ_1 and Γ_2 will be, in general, finite unions of polygons, but still, by addition, $\int_{\Gamma_1} f = \int_{\Gamma_2} f = 0$. Hence the semi-annulus R *is* a polygonally-Cauchy region.

A similar argument shows that if R is an annular sector with radii r_1 and r, where $r_1/r > \sqrt{2}$, and angle $\pi + \varepsilon$, then R is polygonally-Cauchy, for sufficiently small ε. Then we can join two of these together (A and B in Fig. 11) to prove that the "slit annulus" D shown in Fig. 11 is polygonally-Cauchy.

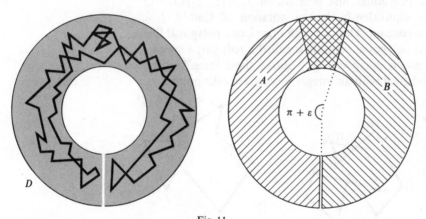

Fig. 11

However, it is easy to see that no *annulus* is polygonally-Cauchy. For example, let $E = \{z : 1 < |z| < 3\}$, and Γ be the square of side 4, as shown in Fig. 12; then $z \longrightarrow 1/z$ is analytic on E and yet $\int_{\Gamma} \frac{1}{z} dz = 2\pi i \neq 0$.

What, then, is the difference between the slit annulus D and the annulus E?

An approximation to the answer is obvious: E has a "hole" in it, whereas D has not. To get more information we should look at this in terms of the polygons we have been using. For the clearest indication we shall consider *simple* polygons.

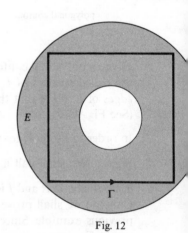

Fig. 12

The difference between D and E can be formulated as follows. For D, every point inside a simple polygon Γ in D also lies in D: for E, there are simple polygons for which this is *not* so. Put more loosely, no polygon in D can wrap round the points in the middle, whereas some polygons in E can (since there is a "hole" in E).

We are on the verge of formulating a definition that will embrace D and exclude E. But one point remains to be cleared up. What do we mean by the "inside" of a simple polygon? For the pleasant figures of elementary geometry it is easy to see what the inside and the outside mean, and it is also easy to define them. For example, the inside of the circle $C = \{z : |z| = 1\}$ is the disc $\{z : |z| < 1\}$ and the outside is $\{z : |z| > 1\}$. Note that the inside and outside are regions, disjoint from each other, whose union is the complement of C, and each having boundary C: also the inside is bounded and the outside is unbounded. A similar situation holds for rectangles, triangles, and so on. For a general simple polygon it is impossible to give a nice formula defining the inside, even though visually one can determine it. In this case we must appeal to the Jordan Curve Theorem, stated in *Unit 4*. We shall repeat it here to refresh your memory. (Note that a simple polygon is the path of some simple-closed arc.)

Theorem 5 of Unit 4 (The Jordan Curve Theorem)

If γ is a simple-closed arc, then the set of points in the plane which do not lie on the path of γ is the union of two disjoint regions. One of these regions is bounded: this we call the *inside* of γ. The other, the *outside*, is unbounded. Each point of the path of γ is a boundary point of either region.

In all cases that can be visually checked these definitions of inside and outside correspond to one's intuition.

Now we can make the major definition of the unit.

Definition

> A region R is called **simply-connected** if whenever Γ is a simple polygon in R the inside of Γ is contained in R.

We shall solve our Task (page 68) by showing that "simply-connected region" is a useful characterization of Cauchy region. Our main aim in this section is to prove that a simply-connected region is Cauchy, the result that we call *Cauchy's Theorem for simply-connected regions*. In the next reading section we shall complete the Task by proving the converse, that a Cauchy region is simply-connected.

Intuitively speaking, a region is simply-connected if it has no holes, cracks or pinpricks contained in its midst. Thus the following regions are simply-connected.

Fig. 13

The following are not simply-connected.

Fig. 14

You should learn to recognize from pictures which regions are simply-connected. Later on, we shall discuss some ways of *proving* that certain regions are simply-connected: note that so far we have *not* proved that any region is simply-connected.

Our proof of Cauchy's Theorem for simply-connected regions will closely mimic the proof of Cauchy's Theorem for star regions in Section 5.3 of *Unit 5*. You might find it beneficial to spend a few minutes glancing over Section 5.3 and consider how it might generalize to this new situation.

As you may now have realized, we shall deduce Cauchy's Theorem from the following result on antiderivatives, which we shall prove as Theorem 4 on page 75.

The Antiderivative Theorem for Simply-connected Regions

Let f be analytic on a simply-connected region R. Then f has an antiderivative on R; that is, there is a function F analytic on R such that

$$F'(z) = f(z), \quad z \in R.$$

Let us now consider how this would be proved. Let z_0 be a fixed point of R. The natural definition of F is $F(z) = \int_\Gamma f$ where Γ is some contour from z_0 to z. Which contour? Well, if R were a star region, with star z_0, we would take Γ to be $[z_0, z]$. Now even though R is not necessarily star, it *is* polygonally-connected, and so we can take Γ to be some polygonal line from z_0 to z. Obviously we cannot fix any *particular* line, so we must prove that the value of $F(z)$ does not depend on the actual line Γ joining z_0 to z. If Γ^* is another polygonal line from z_0 to z (Fig. 15) then $\Gamma + (-\Gamma^*)$ is a polygon, and $\int_\Gamma f = \int_{\Gamma^*} f$ provided that $\int_{\Gamma + (-\Gamma^*)} f = 0$. Thus we have to prove Cauchy's Theorem for polygons.

Γ^*

z_0 Γ

Fig. 15

Let us see if at least we can prove Cauchy's Theorem for *simple* polygons. We have already proved Cauchy's Theorem for a triangle (in *Unit 5*). Thus a useful step might be to decompose a simple polygon into triangles. But this is intuitively obvious: take any simple polygon Γ with more than three sides, and join vertices by lines not crossing any sides, thus decomposing Γ into simple polygons each with fewer sides than Γ—eventually you end up with triangles (Fig. 16). We shall not prove this result because the proof is tedious, but not hard, and has little relevance to our main theme.

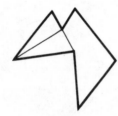

Fig. 16

Recall that a simple polygon is a simple-closed contour, and so carries an *orientation*. If we also take this into account, orientating the triangles appropriately, we end up with the following lemma.

Lemma 1

Let Γ be a simple polygon with n sides (where $n > 3$). Then there are $n - 2$ triangles $T_1, \ldots, T_{n-2}$ with the following properties:

(a)   each point inside a T_j is inside Γ;

(b)   each point inside Γ is inside or on the edge of some T_j;

(c)   each edge of Γ is an edge of some T_j, with the same orientation;

(d)   each edge of each T_j joins vertices of Γ and lies on or inside Γ;

(e)   each edge of a T_j not an edge of Γ is an edge with the opposite orientation of some unique $T_k (k \neq j$ of course).

Such a system $T_1, \ldots, T_{n-2}$ of triangles is called a **triangulation** of Γ. The properties (a)–(e) say no more than can be discerned from the following figure.

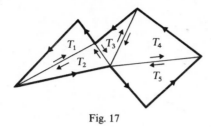

Fig. 17

Note that Γ may have more than one triangulation (see Figs. 17 and 18).

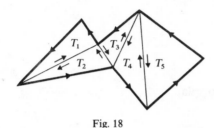

Fig. 18

Now, with the aid of Lemma 1 and the definition of simply-connected, we can prove the first theorem.

Theorem 3   (Cauchy's Theorem for Simple Polygons)

Let R be a simply-connected region, f a function analytic on R, and Γ a simple polygon in R. Then $\int_\Gamma f = 0$.

Proof

We can assume that Γ has $n > 3$ sides (since otherwise Cauchy's Theorem for a triangle applies); so let $T_1, \ldots, T_{n-2}$ be a triangulation of Γ. Since R is simply-connected, the inside of Γ is contained in R, and so (by properties (a) and (d) above) each T_j and its inside are contained in R. Thus by Cauchy's Theorem for a triangle, $\int_{T_j} f = 0$. Now by properties (c) and (e) above,

$$\int_\Gamma f = \int_{T_1} f + \cdots + \int_{T_{n-2}} f$$
$$= 0 + \cdots + 0 = 0. \quad \blacksquare$$

Using this result, we can proceed further towards the Antiderivative Theorem with the help of another lemma, which again is intuitively obvious but tiresome to prove, and, since it is not related to our main theme, we do not prove it.

We require the following definition in order to state the lemma.

We define a *double line* to be a polygonal line of the form $[z_1, z_2, z_1]$, that is, a line segment traversed once in each direction.

Lemma 2

Let Γ be any polygon. Then we can add extra vertices to Γ and find simple polygons $\Gamma_1, \ldots, \Gamma_m$ and double lines $L_1, \ldots, L_n$ such that

(a)   every edge of a Γ_j or L_k is an edge of Γ with the same orientation;

(b)   every edge of Γ is an edge of some Γ_j or L_k with the same orientation.

The process for obtaining the Γ_j and L_k can be described in a sequence of pictures as follows.

(1)   Begin with a polygon Γ.

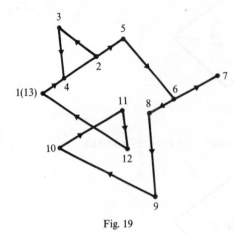

Fig. 19

(2)   Add new vertices wherever edges cross or overlap.

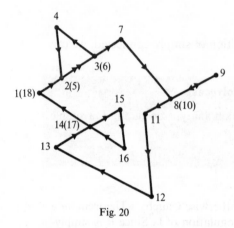

Fig. 20

(3)   Split off the simple polygons Γ_j and double lines L_k as shown.

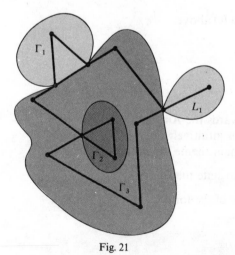

Fig. 21

(This type of argument is often called *combinatorial*. There is a branch of mathematics called "combinatorics".)

Corollary to Theorem 3   (Cauchy's Theorem for Polygons)

Let R be a simply-connected region. Then R is polygonally-Cauchy; that is, if f is analytic on R and Γ is a polygon in R then $\int_{\Gamma} f = 0$.

Proof

By Lemma 2 above, Γ can be decomposed into simple polygons $\Gamma_1, \ldots, \Gamma_m$ and double lines $L_1, \ldots, L_n$. Clearly $\int_{L_k} f = 0$ for each k. Also $\int_{\Gamma_j} f = 0$ since Γ_j is a simple polygon in R (using Theorem 3). Now

$$\int_{\Gamma} f = \int_{\Gamma_1} + \cdots + \int_{\Gamma_m} f + \int_{L_1} f + \cdots + \int_{L_n} f,$$

by the properties of the Γ_j and L_k, and so $\int_{\Gamma} f = 0$. ∎

Now we can carry out the procedure outlined on page 72, to prove the Antiderivative Theorem.

Theorem 4   (The Antiderivative Theorem for Simply-connected Regions)

Let f be analytic on a simply-connected region R. Then f has an antiderivative on R; that is, there is a function F analytic on R such that

$$F'(z) = f(z), \quad z \in R.$$

Proof

Let z_0 be a fixed point of R. Define F on R by $F(z) = \int_{\Gamma} f$ where Γ is *any* polygonal line in R from z_0 to z. Note that there is at least *one* such Γ. If Γ^* is another, then, $\Gamma + (-\Gamma^*)$ is a polygon, and so by the Corollary to Theorem 3, $\int_{\Gamma + (-\Gamma^*)} f = 0$, so that $\int_{\Gamma} f = \int_{\Gamma^*} f$. Hence $F(z)$ is independent of Γ.

Now, for sufficiently small $|h|$,

$$\frac{F(z + h) - F(z)}{h} = \frac{1}{h} \int_{[z, z + h]} f,$$

since if $F(z) = \int_{\Gamma} f$ then $F(z + h) = \int_{\Gamma + [z, z + h]} f$.

Hence

$$F'(z) = \lim_{h \to 0} \frac{1}{h} \int_{[z, z + h]} f$$
$$= f(z),$$

by the estimation argument in the proof of the Antiderivative Theorem in *Unit 5*. ∎

Finally we can deduce Cauchy's Theorem for simply-connected regions.

Theorem 5   (Cauchy's Theorem for Simply-connected Regions)

Let R be a simply-connected region. Then R is a Cauchy region; that is, if f is analytic on R, and Γ is any closed contour in R, then $\int_{\Gamma} f = 0$.

Proof

Let f be analytic on R, and Γ be a closed contour in R. By the Antiderivative Theorem there is F analytic on R such that $F' = f$ on R. Thus

$$\int_\Gamma f = \int_\Gamma F'$$

$$= 0, \quad \text{since } \Gamma \text{ is closed, by the Fundamental Theorem (in } Unit\ 4). \blacksquare$$

Remark on Names of Theorems

In future, when we refer to the Antiderivative Theorem and Cauchy's Theorem,* we shall mean Theorems 4 and 5 of this unit, respectively—the corresponding results in *Unit 5* are now superseded.

There are many consequences of Cauchy's Theorem, in this general form. A simple one is that if Γ_1 and Γ_2 are any two contours (not necessarily polygonal) in R with the same endpoints, then $\int_{\Gamma_1} f = \int_{\Gamma_2} f$ (because $\Gamma = \Gamma_1 + (-\Gamma_2)$ is a closed contour, and so $\int_{\Gamma_1} f - \int_{\Gamma_2} f = \int_\Gamma f = 0$). Thus contour integrals of analytic functions are independent of path in simply-connected regions.

Several other consequences require additional concepts or results, and so will be deferred until later sections. However, there is one example that we shall discuss now.

Example

Let f be analytic and non-zero on a simply-connected region R. Show that there is a function g analytic on R such that $e^{g(z)} = f(z)$, $z \in R$. (We call such a function g an **analytic logarithm of f on R**. If $f(z) = z$, $z \in R$, we call g an **analytic logarithm on R**.)

Solution

If such a g exists, then by differentiating,

$$e^{g(z)} \cdot g'(z) = f'(z);$$

that is,

$$g'(z) = \frac{f'(z)}{f(z)}.$$

This gives us a clue how to *define* such a g. Since f'/f is analytic on R, there is a function F analytic on R such that $F' = f'/f$, by the Antiderivative Theorem. We now have to show that $e^F = f$. If we could show that $(e^F)' = f'$ we would be well on the way, but we cannot establish this directly. However, we could try to show that $e^{-F}f = 1$ by investigating $(e^{-F}f)'$.

Now

$$(e^{-F}f)'(z) = e^{-F(z)}f'(z) - e^{-F(z)}F'(z)f(z)$$

$$= 0, \quad \text{since } F' = f'/f;$$

so that $e^{-F(z)}f(z) = k$ for some constant $k \neq 0$, that is, $f(z) = ke^{F(z)}$. It is easy to adjust F to get rid of the k: choose α such that $e^\alpha = k$, and let $g(z) = F(z) + \alpha$: then $e^{g(z)} = e^{F(z)} e^\alpha = ke^{F(z)} = f(z)$. Thus g is the required function.

---

* Cauchy's original proof in 1825 involved the consideration of the two line integrals obtained by splitting f into real and imaginary parts, and used the hypothesis that f' is continuous. Edouard Goursat (1858–1936) avoided this condition; his proof involved splitting the interior of R into small squares. The proof of the Cauchy–Goursat Theorem (*in Unit 5*), in which Γ is a triangular contour, is due to A. Pringsheim (1850–1941).

In particular we see that for any simply-connected region R not containing 0, there is an analytic logarithm L on R, that is $e^{L(z)} = z$, $z \in R$. Any branch of the logarithm (in the sense of *Unit 3*) is an analytic logarithm. However, the method of the example has given us much more information than we had in *Unit 3*, when we dealt only with cut planes. For example, each of the regions in Fig. 22 has an analytic logarithm defined on it.

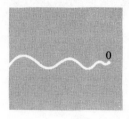 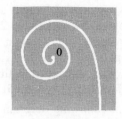 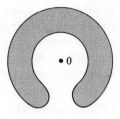

Fig. 22

Once we have an analytic logarithm on a region we can define analytic square roots, and so on (see Problem 2 of the next section). Further discussion of analytic logarithms occurs in *Unit 11, Analytic Functions*.

Summary

This section has been devoted to a proof of Cauchy's Theorem for simply-connected regions. The definition of "simply-connected" is phrased in terms of polygons, and we required two lemmas on polygons, which we did not prove (although we tried to make them seem fairly obvious). We began with Cauchy's Theorem for a triangle (the Cauchy-Goursat Theorem of *Unit 5*). From this, together with Lemma 1 on triangulating simple polygons, we proved Cauchy's Theorem for simple polygons (Theorem 3). From that, together with Lemma 2 on decomposing polygons, we proved Cauchy's Theorem for polygons (Corollary to Theorem 3). This gave us the result on independence of path that we needed for the Antiderivative Theorem (Theorem 4), which, together with the Fundamental Theorem (of *Unit 4*), implied Cauchy's Theorem (Theorem 5).

We can summarize the proof of Cauchy's Theorem by the following diagram.

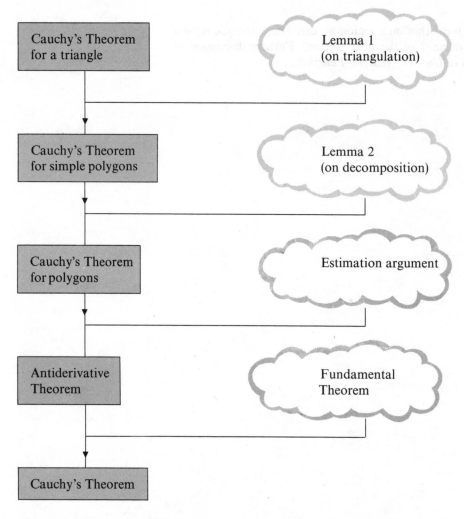

We have completed half of our Task (page 68): we have shown that a simply-connected region is a Cauchy region.

Self-Assessment Questions

1. Define "Cauchy region".

2. Which of the following polygonal lines are (a) polygons and (b) simple polygons?

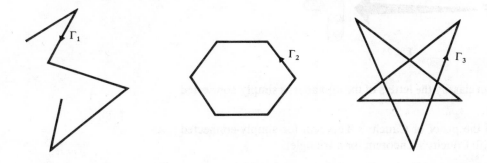

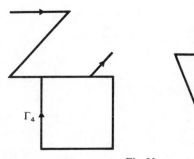

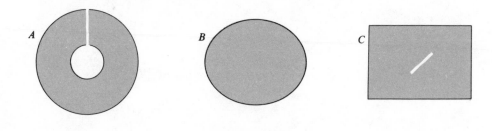

Fig. 23

3. Which of the following regions are simply-connected?

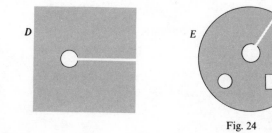

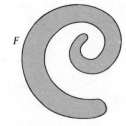

Fig. 24

4. Imagine the capital letters of the alphabet fattened out to regions in the obvious way: thus, for example,

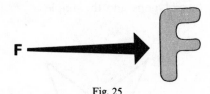

Fig. 25

See how fast you can classify the letters of the alphabet as simply-connected or not.

5. Give an outline of the proof of Cauchy's Theorem for simply-connected regions (starting with Cauchy's Theorem for a triangle).

6. Let R be a simply-connected region, Γ a closed contour in R, and α a point not in R. Why is $\int_{\Gamma} \frac{1}{z - \alpha} dz$ zero?

Solutions

1. A region R is Cauchy if whenever Γ is a closed contour in R and f is analytic on R then $\int_\Gamma f = 0$.

2. (a) Γ_2, Γ_3, and Γ_5 are polygons.

    (b) Γ_2 is a simple polygon.

3. Regions A, B, D and F are simply-connected: the others are not.

4. The easiest way is to write down the alphabet and strike out those letters which are not simply-connected. Then you should get

    A̸ B̸ C D̸ E F G H I J K L M N Ø P̸ Ø R̸ S T U V W X Y Z.

    Thus only 7 are not simply-connected.

5. Let f be analytic on a simply-connected region R.

    (1) If Γ is a simple polygon, then, by Lemma 1 on triangulation, Γ is a "sum" of triangles, and so

    $$\int_\Gamma f = 0.$$

    (Theorem 3)

    (2) If Γ is any polygon, then, by Lemma 2, Γ is a sum of simple polygons and double lines, so again

    $$\int_\Gamma f = 0.$$

    (Corollary to Theorem 3)

    (3) Let $F(z) = \int_\Gamma f$ where Γ is a polygonal contour from z_0 (fixed) to z. Then F is well defined and analytic, with derivative f.

    (Theorem 4)

    (4) If Γ is any closed contour, then

    $$\int_\Gamma f = \int_\Gamma F' = 0,$$

    by the Fundamental Theorem.

    (Theorem 5)

6. Let $f(z) = \dfrac{1}{z - \alpha}$. Then f is analytic on R, and so by Cauchy's Theorem

    $$\int_\Gamma f = 0.$$

9.4 PROBLEMS

1. Prove that the outside of the ellipse $x^2 + 4y^2 = 1$ is not a Cauchy region.

2. Let f be analytic on a region R. We call g an **analytic square root of f on R** if g is analytic on R and $g^2 = f$ on R.

   Let f be analytic and non-zero on a simply-connected region R.

   (a) Find two distinct analytic square roots g_1 and g_2 of f on R.

   (b) Let g be an analytic square root of f on R. By considering the set $\{z \in R : g(z) \neq g_1(z)\}$, show that $g = g_1$ on R or $g = g_2$ on R.

   If f is the identity function, g_1 and g_2 are **analytic square roots on** R. By similar methods, one can construct **analytic cube roots, analytic inverse sines**, and so on.

We have not so far *proved* that any region is simply-connected, although later we shall prove some general results. But it is possible sometimes to prove from first principles that a region is simply-connected. Try the next two problems on this.

---

3. Let R be the complement of the non-negative real axis. Prove that R is simply-connected. (Hint: Let Γ be a simple polygon in R, and consider the least upper bound of those real $t \geqslant 0$, if any, lying inside Γ.)

4. Let $\gamma : [0, \infty] \longrightarrow \mathbb{C}$ be a one-one continuous function such that $\lim\limits_{t \to \infty} |\gamma(t)| = \infty$. Show that the complement of the range of γ is simply-connected.

5. "Combinatorial" arguments with polygonal lines can be used for purposes other than those in the last section. The following result is proved in such a way, and is quite useful. Establishing this result is rather easier than the proof of Lemmas 1 and 2, which we omitted.

   Show that any two points in a region can be joined by a simple polygonal contour. (You have to "disentangle" a polygonal contour. First get a general idea of what to do. Then try to find a systematic way of carrying it out: do not spend too much time on this part of the problem.)

Solutions

1. Let R be the outside of the ellipse. Then the circle C with radius 2 and centre the origin lies in R(Fig. 26). Now $\int_C \frac{1}{z}\,dz = 2\pi i \neq 0$. But $z \longrightarrow \frac{1}{z}$ is analytic on R. Hence R is not Cauchy.

2. (a) By the example on page 76, there is h analytic on R such that $e^{h(z)} = f(z)$, $z \in R$. Let $g_1(z) = e^{h(z)/2}$, $g_2(z) = -e^{h(z)/2}$. Then $[g_1(z)]^2 = e^{2 \cdot h(z)/2} = f(z)$, and similarly $[g_2(z)]^2 = f(z)$. Clearly $g_1(z) \neq g_2(z)$ for all $z \in R$, since $g_1(z) - g_2(z) = 2e^{h(z)/2} \neq 0$.

   (b) Let g be *any* function analytic on R such that $g^2 = f$. Pick $z_0 \in R$. Then $g(z_0) \in \{g_1(z_0), g_2(z_0)\}$, since $f(z_0)$ has exactly two square roots. Let $G_1 = \{z \in R : g(z) \neq g_1(z)\}$, $G_2 = \{z \in R : g(z) \neq g_2(z)\}$. Then G_1 and G_2 are open (being inverse images of open sets), and disjoint, with union R. Hence one of them is empty, since R is connected. If $G_1 = \varnothing$ then $g = g_1$, while if $G_2 = \varnothing$ then $g = g_2$.

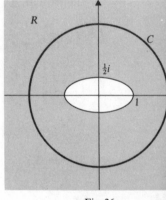

Fig. 26

3. Let Γ be a simple polygon in R. Intuitively, of course, Γ cannot straddle even part of the positive real axis, but you were asked to *prove* this. Suppose that some t_0 inside Γ does not lie in R: then t_0 is a positive real number (Fig. 27).

    Let $G = \{t \in \mathbf{R} : [t_0, t] \text{ lies inside } \Gamma\}$. Then G is nonempty (since $t_0 \in G$) and bounded above (since the inside of Γ is a bounded set). Let α be the least upper bound of G; then α is real and $\alpha \geqslant 0$. If $\alpha \in G$ then α lies inside Γ, and, since the inside of Γ is an open set, α is *not* an upper bound. If $\alpha \notin G$ then α lies outside Γ, and, since the outside of Γ is an open set, α is not the *least* upper bound. This gives a contradiction. (This proof is very similar to Theorem 7 of *Unit 2*, the proof that a convex open set is connected.)

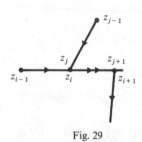

Fig. 27

4. We use an argument very similar to that in Problem 3. Let Γ be any closed contour in the complement of the range of γ. Suppose that $\gamma(t_0)$ lies inside Γ, for some $t_0 \geqslant 0$. Let $G = \{t \in \mathbf{R} : \gamma(s) \text{ lies inside } \Gamma \text{ for all } s \in [t_0, t]\}$. Since Γ is a bounded set, there is some k such that $|z| < k$ for all $z \in \Gamma$, and since $\lim_{t \to \infty} |\gamma(t)| = \infty$, there is t_1 such that $|\gamma(t)| > k$ for all $t \geqslant t_1$. Hence G is bounded above, by t_1; so let α be the least upper bound of G. Suppose $\alpha \in G$. Then $\gamma(\alpha)$ lies inside Γ. But since the inside of Γ is open, there is $\varepsilon > 0$ such that $\{z : |z - \gamma(\alpha)| < \varepsilon\}$ lies inside Γ. Since γ is continuous, there is $\delta > 0$ such that if $|t - \alpha| < \delta$, then $|\gamma(t) - \gamma(\alpha)| < \varepsilon$, and so $\gamma(t)$ lies inside Γ. Hence $\alpha + \frac{1}{2}\delta \in G$ and so α is *not* an upper bound. Similarly, if $\alpha \notin G$ then α is not the *least* upper bound, the outside of Γ being open. This gives a contradiction.

    As applications we see immediately that the following sets are simply-connected.

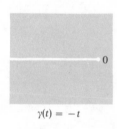

$\gamma(t) = -t$

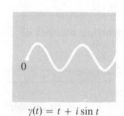

$\gamma(t) = t + i \sin t$

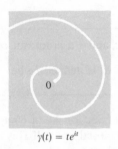

$\gamma(t) = t e^{it}$

Fig. 28

5. Let R be a region, and $a, b \in R$. Let $[z_0, \ldots, z_n]$ be a polygonal contour joining $a = z_0$ to $b = z_n$ in R. As in Lemma 2, by adding finitely many extra points if necessary we can assume that a vertex occurs whenever two lines cross. Thus crossings or overlaps look as in Fig. 29.

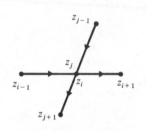
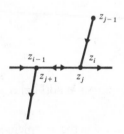

Fig. 29

Let z_i be the first vertex such that $z_i = z_j$ for some $j > i$. There are only two possibilities.

1. z_{j+1} is not z_{i-1}. Then replace $[z_0, \ldots, z_n]$ by $[z_0, \ldots, z_i, z_{j+1}, \ldots, z_n]$, and re-number these vertices.

2. z_{j+1} is z_{i-1}. Then replace $[z_0, \ldots, z_n]$ by $[z_0, \ldots, z_{i-1}, z_{j+2}, \ldots, z_n]$ and re-number these vertices.

Repeat this process—as the number of vertices decreases each time, the process must terminate. The result is a simple polygonal contour joining $z_0 = a$ to $z_n = b$. (Essentially what we are doing here is removing all the loops and double lines that occurred in the original contour.)

You probably appreciate now why we did not prove Lemmas 1 and 2.

9.5 WINDING NUMBER

We have two main aims in this section: to complete our Task (page 68) by proving that every Cauchy region is simply-connected, and to prove a general version of Cauchy's Formula. It turns out that these two aims are related by the topic of winding number, and so we shall begin by discussing this.

Winding Number

The notion of winding number was introduced in *Unit 4* (Problem 7 of Section 4.6), but in case you have forgotten it, we shall repeat the definition here, in a slightly more general context.

Remember that the winding number counts the number of times a curve passes around a point. For curves which are difficult to draw accurately, it is hard to determine this number geometrically. So we start with an abstract definition.

Definition

Let Γ be a closed contour, and α a point not on Γ. The **winding number of** Γ **about** α, written $\text{Wnd}(\Gamma, \alpha)$ is defined to be $\dfrac{1}{2\pi i}\displaystyle\int_{\Gamma} \dfrac{dz}{z - \alpha}$.

It was proved in Problem 7 of Section 4.6 of *Unit 4*, that $\text{Wnd}(\Gamma, \alpha)$ is an integer if Γ is the path of a smooth closed arc γ. If Γ is a closed contour, we can split Γ into paths of smooth closed arcs, and by considering these, prove in a similar way that $\text{Wnd}(\Gamma, \alpha)$ is an integer.

There are three other properties of the function $\alpha \longrightarrow \text{Wnd}(\Gamma, \alpha)$ that one can prove by well-tried methods, and, as we need them later, we have set them as preliminary problems. (They are good revision, as well.)

Preliminary Problems

1. Prove that the function $\alpha \longrightarrow \text{Wnd}(\Gamma, \alpha)$ is continuous on the complement of Γ.

2. Let R be a region contained in the complement of Γ. Prove that the function $\alpha \longrightarrow \text{Wnd}(\Gamma, \alpha)$ is constant on R.

3. Prove that $\text{Wnd}(\Gamma, \alpha) = 0$ for fixed Γ and sufficiently large $|\alpha|$.

Solutions

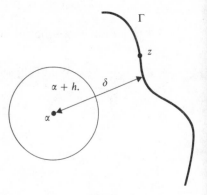

Fig. 30

1. Let S be the complement of Γ. Then S is open (since Γ is closed). Let $\alpha \in S$. If $\alpha + h \in S$ then

$$\text{Wnd}(\Gamma, \alpha + h) - \text{Wnd}(\Gamma, \alpha) = \frac{1}{2\pi i}\left(\int_\Gamma \frac{dz}{z - \alpha - h} - \int_\Gamma \frac{dz}{z - \alpha} \right)$$

$$= \frac{1}{2\pi i} \int_\Gamma \frac{h}{(z - \alpha - h)(z - \alpha)} dz.$$

Let δ be the distance from α to Γ (Fig. 30). If $|h| < \frac{1}{2}\delta$ then $|z - \alpha - h| > \frac{1}{2}\delta$ for z on Γ, and so

$$|\text{Wnd}(\Gamma, \alpha + h) - \text{Wnd}(\Gamma, \alpha)| \leqslant \frac{1}{2\pi} \frac{L}{\frac{1}{2}\delta \cdot \delta} |h|, \quad \text{where } L \text{ is the length of } \Gamma,$$

$$= \frac{L}{\pi\delta^2} |h|,$$

which has limit 0 as h approaches 0.

Thus $\lim_{h \to 0} \text{Wnd}(\Gamma, \alpha + h) = \text{Wnd}(\Gamma, \alpha)$, for all $\alpha \in S$: that is, $\alpha \longrightarrow \text{Wnd}(\Gamma, \alpha)$ is continuous on S.

2. Pick $\alpha_0 \in R$ and let $k = \text{Wnd}(\Gamma, \alpha_0)$ Now

$$R = G_1 \cup G_2 \quad \text{and} \quad G_1 \cap G_2 = \varnothing,$$

where $G_1 = \{z \in R : \text{Wnd}(\Gamma, z) = k\}$ and $G_2 = \{z \in R : \text{Wnd}(\Gamma, z) \neq k\}$. Clearly G_2 is open. Now since $\text{Wnd}(\Gamma, z)$ is an integer for all z, $G_1 = \{z \in R : |\text{Wnd}(\Gamma, z) - k| < \frac{1}{2}\}$, and so G_1 is open. Since R is connected and $G_1 \neq \varnothing$, $R = G_1$.

3. This is an estimation argument: note that we need prove only that $|\text{Wnd}(\Gamma, \alpha)| \leqslant \frac{1}{2}$. (Of course, any number less than one would do.) Now

$$|\text{Wnd}(\Gamma, \alpha)| = \frac{1}{2\pi} \left| \int_\Gamma \frac{dz}{z - \alpha} \right|.$$

Let Γ have length L and be bounded by k. Then

$$|\text{Wnd}(\Gamma, \alpha)| \leqslant \frac{1}{2\pi} \frac{L}{|\alpha| - k}, \quad \text{if } |\alpha| > k,$$

$$\leqslant \tfrac{1}{2}, \quad \text{if } |\alpha| > k + \frac{L}{\pi}.$$

These results are all very well, but the definition of winding number is at present not amenable to intuition. However, we can reformulate it in a more geometrical way, as follows. For simplicity let $\alpha = 0$ and Γ be the path of a smooth closed arc $\gamma : [a, b] \longrightarrow \mathbb{C}$. (In fact, Γ can be any closed contour.) To begin with, we repeat the calculations of Problem 7 in Section 4.6 of *Unit 4*.

Let $l(x) = \int_a^x \frac{\gamma'(t)}{\gamma(t)} dt$, $a \leqslant x \leqslant b$, and $\gamma(x) \neq 0$ for $x \in [a, b]$. If $m(x) = e^{-l(x)}\gamma(x)$, then

$$m'(x) = e^{-l(x)}(\gamma'(x) - l'(x)\gamma(x))$$

$$= 0, \quad \text{since } l'(x) = \gamma'(x)/\gamma(x).$$

Hence $m(x) = k$ for some constant k. Clearly $k = e^{-l(x)}\gamma(x) \neq 0$. Let λ be a logarithm of k (that is, $e^\lambda = k$), and let $L(x) = l(x) + \lambda$. Then

$$e^{L(x)} = e^{l(x)}e^\lambda = ke^{l(x)} = \gamma(x),$$

so that $L(x)$ is a logarithm of $\gamma(x)$ for all $x \in [a, b]$. Since L is continuous, we call it a **continuous logarithm of** γ.

Now we go on to define a continuous argument. (You probably have an intuitive idea of what this is: namely, that the argument of a point which varies continuously as the point moves along a curve. But are you confident that your intuitive idea is applicable to curves you cannot draw?) So we define the function $A : [a, b] \longrightarrow \mathbb{C}$ by $A(x) = -i[L(x) - \log|\gamma(x)|]$, $x \in (a, b)$, which on rearranging gives $L(x) = \log|\gamma(x)| + iA(x)$; hence A is continuous. Also, since $L(x)$ is a logarithm of $\gamma(x)$, $L(x) = \log|\gamma(x)| + i\theta$ where θ is an argument of $\gamma(x)$; hence $A(x) = \theta$ and so $A(x)$ is an argument of $\gamma(x)$. We call A a **continuous argument of** γ.

Finally, we show that $\text{Wnd}(\Gamma, 0) = \dfrac{1}{2\pi}[A(b) - A(a)]$. This is easy, since

$$
\begin{aligned}
\text{Wnd}(\Gamma, 0) &= \frac{1}{2\pi i}\int_\gamma \frac{dz}{z} \\
&= \frac{1}{2\pi i}\int_a^b \frac{\gamma'(t)}{\gamma(t)}\,dt \\
&= \frac{1}{2\pi i}[l(b) - l(a)] \\
&= \frac{1}{2\pi i}[L(b) - L(a)] \\
&= \frac{1}{2\pi i}[\log|\gamma(b)| + iA(b) - \log|\gamma(a)| - iA(a)] \\
&= \frac{1}{2\pi}[A(b) - A(a)], \quad \text{since } \gamma(b) = \gamma(a).
\end{aligned}
$$

In words, the winding number of Γ about 0 is $\dfrac{1}{2\pi}$ times the difference between the final and initial values of the continuous argument of γ. It is fairly easy to calculate values of the continuous argument and hence the winding number when given a picture of a contour. Here is one example.

Example 1

Determine from the diagram the continuous argument at the points $z_1, \ldots, z_7$ given on the contour Γ in Fig. 31. Hence calculate $\text{Wnd}(\Gamma, 0)$.

Solution

The values at $z_1, \ldots, z_7$ are $0, \dfrac{\pi}{2}, \dfrac{\pi}{2}, 0, \dfrac{\pi}{2}, \dfrac{3\pi}{2}, 2\pi$; final argument − initial argument $= 2\pi$. Hence the winding number is 1.

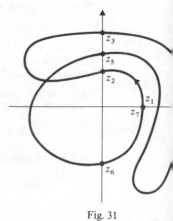

Fig. 31

Problem 4

Determine from the diagrams the winding number of Γ about 0 when Γ is as shown in the following four cases.

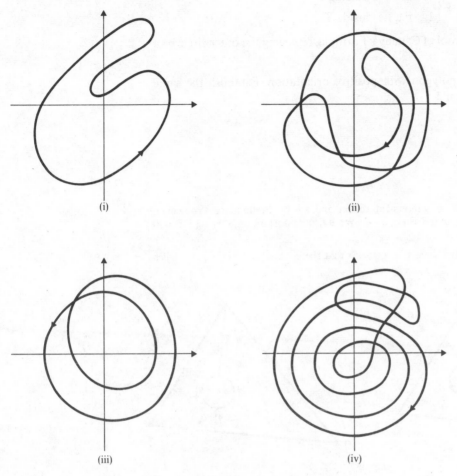

Fig. 32

Solution

(i) 1;   (ii) -1;   (iii) 2;   (iv) -4.

Although pictures can be useful in practical work, when it comes to theoretical results about winding numbers we are very short of *proofs* that winding numbers of contours have certain values, except for the application of Cauchy's Formula in *Unit 5*, which proved that the winding number of a (positively orientated) circle about any point inside it is 1. In view of the previous reading section we should start with a triangle and next consider a simple polygon. Try the next two problems on these.

Problems

5. Let T be a (positively orientated simple) triangle. Prove that

$$\mathrm{Wnd}(T, \alpha) = \begin{cases} 0, & \text{if } \alpha \text{ lies outside } T \\ 1, & \text{if } \alpha \text{ lies inside } T. \end{cases}$$

   (Hint: Mimic the proof of Cauchy's Formula, replacing the outer circle by a triangle.)

6. Let Γ be a simple polygon with positive orientation. Establish the same result as for Problem 5.

Solutions

5. The outside S of T is an unbounded region and so, by Preliminary Problem 3, $\mathrm{Wnd}(T, \alpha) = 0$ for *some* α in S. Since $z \longrightarrow \mathrm{Wnd}(T, z)$ is constant on S, $\mathrm{Wnd}(T, \alpha) = 0$ for *all* α in S.

   Now fix α inside T. Then there is $\varepsilon > 0$ such that the circle $C = \{z : |z - \alpha| = \varepsilon\}$ lies inside T.

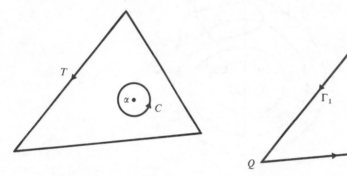

Fig. 33

Draw the line through some vertex P of T and the point α and let it meet the opposite side QR at P'. Let Γ_1 and Γ_2 be the closed contours shown in Fig. 33. Now Γ_1 lies in a star region R_1 (Fig. 34) on which $z \longrightarrow \dfrac{1}{z - \alpha}$ is analytic, so that $\displaystyle\int_{\Gamma_1} \frac{dz}{z - \alpha} = 0$. Similarly, $\displaystyle\int_{\Gamma_2} \frac{dz}{z - \alpha} = 0$. Thus $\displaystyle\int_T \frac{dz}{z - \alpha} - \int_C \frac{dz}{z - \alpha} = 0 + 0$, and so $\mathrm{Wnd}(T, \alpha) = \mathrm{Wnd}(C, \alpha) = 1$.

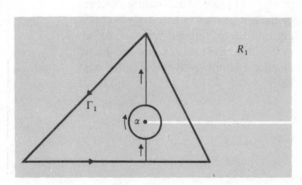

Fig. 34

6. Let Γ be a simple polygon, which we can assume is not a triangle. If α lies outside Γ, the same argument as in Problem 5 shows that $\mathrm{Wnd}(\Gamma, \alpha) = 0$. Let $T_1, \ldots, T_{n-2}$ be a triangulation of Γ. Let α be inside Γ.

(a) Suppose α lies inside T_j. Then $\mathrm{Wnd}(T_j, \alpha) = 1$, whereas $\mathrm{Wnd}(T_k, \alpha) = 0$ for $k \neq j$ (since α lies outside T_k).

Hence $\mathrm{Wnd}(\Gamma, \alpha) = \sum\limits_{k=1}^{n-2} \mathrm{Wnd}(T_k, \alpha) = 1$.

(b) Suppose α lies on an edge of some T_j (Fig. 35).

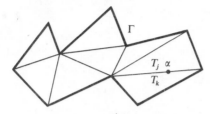

Fig. 35

Then α lies also on an edge of some T_k, $k \neq j$. For β inside T_j or inside T_k, $\mathrm{Wnd}(\Gamma, \beta) = 1$.

Since $z \longrightarrow \mathrm{Wnd}(\Gamma, z)$ is continuous, $\mathrm{Wnd}(\Gamma, \alpha) = 1$.

With this result on the winding number of a polygon, we can now complete our Task (page 68), by proving that any Cauchy region is simply-connected.

Theorem 6

If R is a Cauchy region then R is simply-connected.

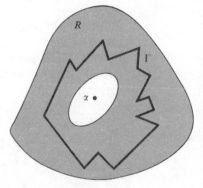

Fig. 36

Proof

Suppose that R is a Cauchy region, but that R is not simply-connected. Then there is a simple polygon Γ in R (which we can assume has positive orientation), and a point α inside Γ such that $\alpha \notin R$ (Fig. 36). Thus $z \longrightarrow 1/(z - \alpha)$ is analytic on R, so that $\int_\Gamma \dfrac{1}{z - \alpha} dz = 0$, since R is a Cauchy region. But by Problem 6, $\mathrm{Wnd}(\Gamma, \alpha) = 1$ (since α lies inside Γ) and so $\int_\Gamma \dfrac{1}{z - \alpha} dz = 2\pi i$. This is a contradiction. ∎

This result is not just of theoretical interest. Recall that, apart from Problems 3 and 4 of the previous section, we have no general methods of proving that a region is simply-connected. But since any star region is Cauchy (by Cauchy's Theorem for star regions), we have the following important corollary of Theorem 6.

Corollary

Every star region is simply-connected.

This corollary is reassuring, but not very surprising—there would have been something seriously wrong with our definition of "simply-connected" if it had not held.

There is one last general theorem yielding simply-connected regions. We cannot prove it, since the proof "comes out in the wash" when proving the Jordan Curve Theorem. In mathematical parlance, it is called a "rider" to that theorem.

Rider to the Jordan Curve Theorem

Let Γ be the path of a simple-closed arc. Then the inside of Γ is simply-connected.

In particular, the regions in Fig. 37 are all simply-connected. In fact, you will not go far wrong if you think of the inside of a simple-closed contour when visualizing a "typical" simply-connected region.

  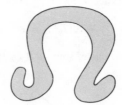

Fig. 37

Cauchy's Formula

Now we move on to the second topic of this section, Cauchy's Formula. Recall that in *Unit 5*, we proved Cauchy's Formula for a circle, which stated that for a circle Γ,

$$f(\alpha) = \frac{1}{2\pi i}\int_{\Gamma} \frac{f(z)}{z - \alpha}dz, \quad \text{for } \alpha \text{ inside } \Gamma,$$

under certain conditions on f. We shall now prove the analogue of this for a general closed contour. The advantage of doing this is that the result is so general that its proof is easy, and furthermore that the result points the way to more specific results. (These advantages do not always occur with general results!)

Theorem 7 (Cauchy's Formula for a Closed Contour)

Let f be analytic on a simply-connected region R, Γ a closed contour in R, and α a point in R not on Γ. Then

$$\frac{1}{2\pi i}\int_{\Gamma} \frac{f(z)}{z - \alpha}dz = Nf(\alpha), \quad \text{where } N = \text{Wnd}(\Gamma, \alpha).$$

Proof

Since $N = \dfrac{1}{2\pi i}\displaystyle\int_{\Gamma} \dfrac{dz}{z - \alpha}$,

$$\frac{1}{2\pi i}\int_{\Gamma} \frac{f(z)}{z - \alpha}dz - Nf(\alpha) = \frac{1}{2\pi i}\left(\int_{\Gamma} \frac{f(z)}{z - \alpha}dz - \int_{\Gamma} \frac{f(\alpha)}{z - \alpha}dz\right)$$

$$= \frac{1}{2\pi i}\int_{\Gamma} \frac{f(z) - f(\alpha)}{z - \alpha}dz.$$

Now α is a removable singularity of the function $z \longrightarrow \dfrac{f(z) - f(\alpha)}{z - \alpha}$, by the Lemma to Theorem 1 in *Unit 8, Laurent Series*, and so the function ϕ defined by

$$\phi(z) = \begin{cases} \dfrac{f(z) - f(\alpha)}{z - \alpha}, & z \neq \alpha \\ f'(\alpha), & z = \alpha \end{cases}$$

is analytic on R. Thus

$$\frac{1}{2\pi i}\int_{\Gamma} \frac{f(z) - f(\alpha)}{z - \alpha}dz = \frac{1}{2\pi i}\int_{\Gamma} \phi(z)\,dz$$

$$= 0, \text{ since } R \text{ is simply-connected.}$$

The result follows immediately. ∎

90

In order to derive more specific consequences from this, it is clear that we need to prove results about winding numbers. Now it is intuitively obvious that the winding number of a positively orientated simple-closed contour about a point inside it is 1. We shall now *prove* this. Note that the proof supersedes the results of Problem 5 and 6 earlier, but these were in fact good practice for this more general proof.

Theorem 8

Let Γ be a simple-closed contour, $\alpha \in \Gamma$. Then the winding number of Γ about α satisfies

$$\text{Wnd}(\Gamma, \alpha) = \begin{cases} \pm 1, & \text{if } \alpha \text{ lies inside } \Gamma \\ 0, & \text{if } \alpha \text{ lies outside } \Gamma. \end{cases}$$

Proof

Let R_2 be the outside of Γ. Since $\text{Wnd}(\Gamma, \alpha) = 0$ for all sufficiently large α (by Preliminary Problem 3) and R_2 is unbounded, $\text{Wnd}(\Gamma, \alpha) = 0$ for *some* $\alpha \in R_2$, and so $\text{Wnd}(\Gamma, \alpha) = 0$ for *all* $\alpha \in R_2$ (since $z \longrightarrow \text{Wnd}(\Gamma, \alpha)$ is constant on the region R_2).

Now let R_1 be the inside of Γ, and let $\alpha \in R_1$. Let C be a circle centre α such that C and its inside lie in R_1 (this is possible since α is an interior point of R_1). We shall specify the orientation of C shortly.

Let L be any line through α and let P, Q be the points on either side of α at which it first meets Γ (Fig. 38). (Note that if ϕ is a parametrization of L with $\phi(0) = \alpha$ then $\{t \in \mathbf{R} : t \geqslant 0 \text{ and } \phi(t) \in \Gamma\}$ is a closed subset of $\mathbf{R}$ and so contains its greatest lower bound t_0, by an easy argument. Let P be $\phi(t_0)$. A similar method works for Q.) Let Γ_1 and Γ_2 be the contours as shown in Fig. 38. Since Γ_1 is a simple-closed contour, the outside of Γ_1 is a region. Thus by Problem 5 of the previous section there is a simple polygonal contour from α to a point β far from Γ, say, such that $|\beta| \geqslant |z|$ for all $z \in \Gamma$. We can arrange to add a semi-infinite line segment from β as shown in Fig. 39.

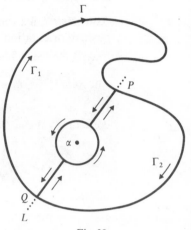

Fig. 38

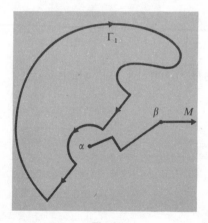

Fig. 39

Let M be that whole curve "from α to ∞". Then the complement of M in $\mathbf{C}$ is simply-connected by Problem 4 of the previous section, and so $\int_{\Gamma_1} \dfrac{dz}{z - \alpha} = 0$.

Similarly, $\int_{\Gamma_2} \dfrac{dz}{z - \alpha} = 0$. Choose the orientation of C so that it is opposite to that induced on the circle by Γ_1 and Γ_2.

Then $\int_{\Gamma} \dfrac{dz}{z - \alpha} - \int_{C} \dfrac{dz}{z - \alpha} = \int_{\Gamma_1} \dfrac{dz}{z - \alpha} + \int_{\Gamma_2} \dfrac{dz}{z - \alpha} = 0$, and so

$$\int_{\Gamma} \frac{dz}{z - \alpha} = \int_{C} \frac{dz}{z - \alpha}.$$

91

But C is traversed either in the positive direction, in which case we have

$$\frac{1}{2\pi i}\int_C \frac{dz}{z-\alpha} = 1, \text{ or in the negative direction, in which case } \frac{1}{2\pi i}\int_C \frac{dz}{z-\alpha} = -1.$$

Hence $\dfrac{1}{2\pi i}\displaystyle\int_\Gamma \dfrac{dz}{z-\alpha} = \pm 1.$ ∎

If you look back to *Unit 4* you will see that we did not give a proper definition of the orientation of a simple-closed contour. But now we can: we say that a simple-closed contour Γ has *positive orientation* if the winding number of Γ about some point inside it is $+1$. (Note that if $\mathrm{Wnd}(\Gamma, \alpha) = 1$ for *some* α inside Γ then $\mathrm{Wnd}(\Gamma, \alpha) = 1$ for *all* α inside Γ.) Similarly, we say that Γ has *negative orientation* if $\mathrm{Wnd}(\Gamma, \alpha) = -1$ for some α inside Γ.

As in *Unit 4*, if a simple-closed contour Γ is given, we shall presume that it has positive orientation, unless otherwise stated. Now by using Theorems 7 and 8, we can deduce a special case of Cauchy's Formula.

Theorem 9   (Cauchy's Formula for a Simple-closed Contour)

Let f be analytic on a simply-connected region R containing a simple-closed contour Γ. Then

$$f(\alpha) = \frac{1}{2\pi i}\int_\Gamma \frac{f(z)}{z-\alpha}\,dz, \quad \alpha \text{ inside } \Gamma.$$

Proof

By Theorem 7, $Nf(\alpha) = \dfrac{1}{2\pi i}\displaystyle\int_\Gamma \dfrac{f(z)}{z-\alpha}\,dz.$ By Theorem 8, $N = \mathrm{Wnd}(\Gamma, \alpha) = 1$ for α inside Γ. ∎

As you would expect from *Unit 5*, we can use Cauchy's Formula to evaluate contour integrals. Here is one example.

Example 2

Evaluate $\displaystyle\int_C \frac{\sin z}{z^2 - 1}\,dz$, where C is

(i)   the ellipse $x^2 + 4y^2 = 4$,

(ii)   the square with vertices $\frac{1}{2} + \frac{1}{2}i$, $\frac{1}{2} - \frac{1}{2}i$, $-\frac{1}{2} + \frac{1}{2}i$ and $-\frac{1}{2} - \frac{1}{2}i$, which may be written $\pm\frac{1}{2} \pm \frac{1}{2}i$.

Solution

Note that

$$\int_C \frac{\sin z}{z^2 - 1}\,dz = \int_C \frac{\sin z}{(z-1)(z+1)}\,dz$$

$$= \frac{1}{2}\int_C \frac{\sin z}{z-1}\,dz - \frac{1}{2}\int_C \frac{\sin z}{z+1}\,dz.$$

We apply Theorems 7 and 9, with $f(z) = \sin z$ and $R = \mathbf{C}$.

(i)   Both -1 and 1 lie inside C (Fig. 40). Thus by Theorem 9,

$$\int_C \frac{\sin z}{z-1}\,dz = \frac{1}{2}\cdot 2\pi i \sin 1 - \frac{1}{2}\cdot 2\pi i \sin(-1)$$

$$= 2\pi i \sin 1.$$

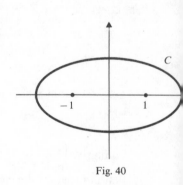

Fig. 40

(ii) Both -1 and 1 lie outside C (Fig. 41), and so $\mathrm{Wnd}(C, -1) = \mathrm{Wnd}(C, 1) = 0$.

Thus by Theorem 7,

$$\int_C \frac{\sin z}{z - 1} dz = \int_C \frac{\sin z}{z + 1} dz = 2\pi i \cdot 0 = 0,$$

and so $\displaystyle\int_C \frac{\sin z}{z^2 - 1} dz = 0.$

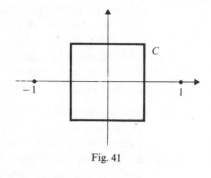

Fig. 41

Note that whatever simple-closed contour C we use in this example, the answer depends only on which of -1 and 1 lie inside C—thus there are at most four possible answers.

If we want to calculate an integral such as $\displaystyle\int_C \frac{\sin z}{(z - 1)^2} dz$, we shall have to use a version of Cauchy's Formula for derivatives (as you would expect from *Unit 5*). This will be established in Problem 1 in the next section. Thus we end up with a method of calculating $\displaystyle\int_C \frac{f(z)}{p(z)} dz$ where f is entire and p is a polynomial, and clearly the values we get for different C depend *only* on which zeros of p lie inside C. But these zeros are just the *singularities* of the function f/p. Thus you might suspect that all this rigmarole with Cauchy's Formulas is just a special case of a method of calculating integrals $\displaystyle\int_C g$ by investigating the singularities of g. In fact, you would be right. The method will be explained in the next reading section, and this is why we have not dwelt overmuch on the above technique, which is now on the verge of obsolescence.

The Jordan Curve Theorem

(If you are interested in the Jordan Curve Theorem, and have the time, read on. If not, go straight to the Summary.) We can summarize the statement of the Jordan Curve Theorem in the following way: every simple-closed arc has an inside and an outside. Thus it has a deceptively simple statement, but is extremely hard to prove. The hardness of the proof is made more exasperating by the fact that, for the simple-closed arcs one can easily draw, the result seems obvious.

But just how obvious is it? Put another way: just how good is the intuitive evidence for the Jordan Curve Theorem? For a curve such as that in Fig. 42 it is easy to determine the inside and outside, and not very hard for a curve such as that in Fig. 43. But what about a really complicated curve, such as that in Fig. 44. Is the point indicated by the cross inside or outside?

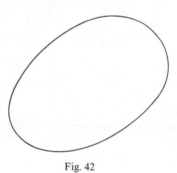

Fig. 42

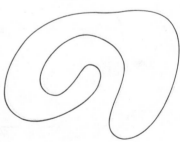

Fig. 43

Fig. 44

Think of the way you might determine the inside of a curve such as the one in Fig. 44. You start at some point far away from the curve—that is, definitely outside. You then colour green, say, all the points that can be reached from the starting point by lines not meeting the curve. Gradually, a sea of green washes over large parts of the picture until it cannot reach any further. That we call the outside. All other points not on the curve are "inside".

But if you work out how to carry out that procedure systematically, say by creeping along close to the curve, rather in the way one might try to get out of a maze, you will see that you have to make certain assumptions about the curve, such as that it is differentiable, has finite length, has not too many spirals, and so on, in order to get finished at all. We cannot really *draw* curves violating such assumptions, but then we are not justified in extrapolating our intuitive ideas to these.

It is fairly easy to construct non-differentiable simple-closed arcs by limiting processes rather similar to those used to construct non-differentiable real functions and space-filling arcs (see Chapter 23 of **Spivak** and *Unit M231 15, Uniform Convergence*). For example, we can construct the so-called *snowflake curve* in the following way.

Consider an equilateral triangle ABC, with sides of length 1 (Fig. 45). Let this be the path of $\gamma_0 : [0, 3] \longrightarrow \mathbf{C}$, where $|\gamma_0'(t)| = 1$. By trisecting each side, construct equilateral triangles DEF, GHJ, KLM, each of side $\frac{1}{3}$; by deleting the lines DF, GJ, and KM we obtain the simple-closed arc $ADE \ldots LMA$ (Fig. 45). Let this be the path of $\gamma_1 : [0, 3] \longrightarrow \mathbf{C}$, with $|\gamma_1'(t)| = \frac{4}{3}$ (so that $\gamma_1(1) = \gamma_0(1) = B$). Continue this process indefinitely, to construct simple-closed arcs

$$\gamma_n : [0, 3] \longrightarrow \mathbf{C}, \quad n \in \mathbf{N}.$$

Let $\gamma(t) = \lim_{n \to \infty} \gamma_n(t)$, $t \in [0, 3]$. Then γ is a simple-closed non-differentiable arc. Can you tell which points are inside γ and which outside?

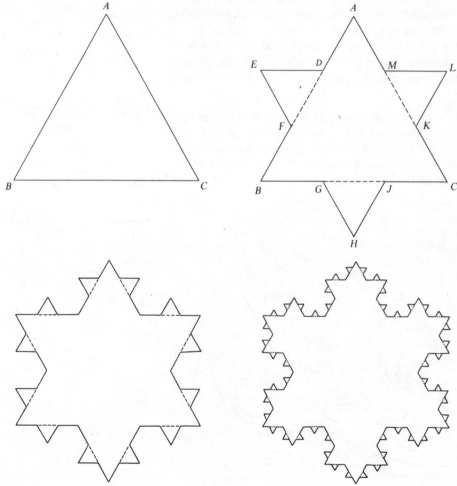

Fig. 45

Unfortunately, though, we do not make the proof of the Jordan Curve Theorem much easier if we insist that γ is a smooth arc, since there are yet other complications which can occur.

Another simplification might occur to you. Curves that can be drawn have the important property that any straight line meets them in a finite number of points and line segments. Curves with this property are of some theoretical interest. For example, they crop up in results like the Repeated Integral Theorem in the Appendix to *Unit M231 9, Properties of the Integral*, and one can give a proof of Cauchy's Theorem for such curves by a bisection argument. It is possible to give a definition of the inside of such a curve Γ which looks relatively straightforward: we say that a point α is inside Γ if any line segment L joining α to a point β far from Γ crosses Γ at an odd number of points. (If one imagines Γ as a sheet of glass which has the peculiar property of changing green light to red and red to green when it passes through the glass, and β as a green sun, then the green points are outside and the red inside.) However, this definition is not free from complexities, such as what to do when L *touches* Γ, and so on.

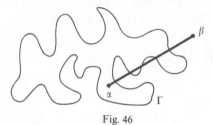

Fig. 46

In fact, the only good definition of the inside of a simple-closed arc, other than "that region prescribed by the Jordan Curve Theorem", is as the set of α with $\text{Wnd}(\Gamma, \alpha) = \pm 1$. However, one cannot get far into the proof of the Jordan Curve Theorem using this alone, and, to be frank, it is not much use as the definition of the inside until we know from the Jordan Curve Theorem that there *is* an inside.

There is no alternative in an elementary complex analysis course to assuming the Jordan Curve Theorem, even though it does look a bit like using a sledgehammer to crack a nut. For some results of complex analysis it could be avoided, by some restatement perhaps, but since it is true, this seems a little pointless.

In fact, for the simple sorts of curve that crop up in practice, it would usually be possible to give a "one-off" proof of the Jordan Curve Theorem. You have done this for an ellipse in *Unit 4* (Problem 5 of Section 4.4), and, more generally, for a polar arc in *Unit 5* (Problem 7 of Section 5.2).

Summary

We began the section by recalling the definition of winding number, and asking you to prove some results on it. We then constructed the continuous argument and discussed the interpretation of winding number in terms of this notion.

After asking you to prove the natural results on winding numbers of simple polygons, we used these to prove the important theorem that a Cauchy region is simply-connected. This theorem completed the Task of Section 9.3. An important corollary was that a star region is simply-connected. We also observed that, in fact, the inside of any simple-closed arc was simply-connected.

We then moved on to Cauchy's Formula. First we proved Cauchy's Formula for an arbitrary closed contour, by integrating the "difference quotient" of an analytic function. Next came the theorem that the winding number of a simple-closed contour about any point inside it is ± 1, which was rather similar to the earlier proof for a triangle, except that a straight cut to give a star region was replaced by a "polygonal cut" to give a simply-connected region. Finally we combined Cauchy's Formula and the winding number result to prove Cauchy's Formula for a simple-closed contour.

We concluded with some more information on the Jordan Curve Theorem, to be read only if you were interested.

Self-Assessment Questions

1. Define "winding number".

2. What is the interpretation of the winding number of a closed contour Γ about a point α in terms of the continuous argument?

3. How would you prove that an open disc is simply-connected?

4. Describe precisely how the winding number of an arbitrary simple-closed contour about a point varies with the position of the point.

5. Write down Cauchy's Formula for a simple-closed contour Γ, stating any other assumptions required.

6. Evaluate the following:

   (i) $\displaystyle \int_C \frac{e^z}{z} dz$, where C is a rectangle with vertices $\pm 2 \pm i$.

   (ii) $\displaystyle \int_C \frac{\tan z}{z - \pi/4} dz$, where C is the triangle with vertices $1, i, -i$.

Solutions

1. The winding number of a closed contour Γ about a point α not on Γ is
$$\frac{1}{2\pi i}\int_\Gamma \frac{dz}{z-\alpha}.$$

2. Let A be a continuous argument of $\gamma - \alpha$, where $\gamma:[a,b] \longrightarrow \mathbf{C}$ is a parametrization of Γ. Then
$$\text{Wnd}(\Gamma, \alpha) = \frac{1}{2\pi}[A(b) - A(a)].$$

3. Any open disc is a star region, and hence a Cauchy region, by Cauchy's Theorem for star regions, and so simply-connected, by Theorem 6.

4. Let Γ be a simple-closed contour. Then $\text{Wnd}(\Gamma, \alpha) = 0$ for all α outside Γ, and either $\text{Wnd}(\Gamma, \alpha) = 1$ for all α inside Γ, or $\text{Wnd}(\Gamma, \alpha) = -1$ for all α inside Γ.

5. $f(\alpha) = \dfrac{1}{2\pi i}\int_\Gamma \dfrac{f(z)}{z-\alpha}dz,$

    where Γ lies in a simply-connected region on which f is analytic, and α lies inside Γ.

6. (i) $2\pi i \cdot e^0 = 2\pi i$ (since 0 lies inside C).

    (ii) $2\pi i \cdot \tan\dfrac{\pi}{4} = 2\pi i \left(\text{since } \dfrac{\pi}{4} \text{ lies inside } C\right).$

9.6 PROBLEMS

1. Prove **Cauchy's Formula for derivatives**:

    Whenever f is analytic on a simply-connected region R, Γ is a simple-closed contour in R, and α is inside Γ, then

    $$f^{(n)}(\alpha) = \frac{n!}{2\pi i} \int_{\Gamma} \frac{f(z)}{(z-\alpha)^{n+1}} \, dz, \quad n \geqslant 0.$$

    (Hint: Look back to Section 5.5 of *Unit 5*—it is enough to indicate how to modify the proof found there.)

2. Evaluate $\int_C \dfrac{e^z}{z^4 - 1} \, dz$, where C is

    (i)   the ellipse $x^2 + 16y^2 = 4$;

    (ii) the rectangle with vertices $\pm \frac{1}{2} \pm 2i$.

3. In this problem we shall prove that the image of a simply-connected region under an analytic function is simply-connected, under certain conditions.

    Let R_1 and R_2 be regions, f a one-one function analytic on its domain R_1, which has range R_2 and an analytic inverse $g : R_2 \longrightarrow R_1$. Suppose also that R_1 is simply-connected.

    (i)   Prove that g' is nonzero on R_2.

    (ii) Let γ be a smooth arc in R_2 with domain $[a, b]$. Prove that

    $$\int_{g \circ \gamma} h \circ f = \int_{\gamma} h \cdot g',$$

    where h is analytic on R_2. (See Problem 3 of Section 4.6 of *Unit 4*.)

    (iii) State and prove the analogous result for contours.

    (iv) Prove that $\int_{\Gamma} h \cdot g' = 0$ for all functions h analytic on R_2 and all closed contours Γ in R_2.

    (v)   Now prove that R_2 is Cauchy, and so simply-connected.

    The next problem gives an application of this.

4. Show that any annular sector (including the slit annulus) is simply-connected.

    (Hint: Try exp.)

5. You can now complete the proof of Theorem 8 of *Unit 8* (Laurent's Theorem for an annulus), by proving *Cauchy's Formula for an annulus*. (Refer to *Unit 8* (page 43) for an explanation of why it is sufficient to prove this.)

    Let A be the annulus $\{\zeta : r_1 < |\zeta - \alpha| < r_2\}$, z be a point in A, and C_1 and C_2 be the circles $|\zeta - \alpha| = \rho_1$ and $|\zeta - \alpha| = \rho_2$ respectively, where $r_1 < \rho_1 < |z - \alpha| < \rho_2 < r_2$. If f is analytic on A, prove that

    $$f(z) = \frac{1}{2\pi i} \int_{C_2} \frac{f(\zeta)}{\zeta - z} \, d\zeta - \frac{1}{2\pi i} \int_{C_1} \frac{f(\zeta)}{\zeta - z} \, d\zeta.$$

    (Hint: By cuts, reduce this to Cauchy's Formula for certain simple-closed contours, and apply the previous problem.)

6. Let γ be a smooth arc, polar about α. Prove that the winding number of γ about α is 1. (Recall that γ is polar about α if $\gamma(\theta) = f(\theta)e^{i\theta} + \alpha$, where f is a positive real function with domain $[0, 2\pi]$ and $f(0) = f(2\pi)$. Express $\text{Wnd}(\Gamma, \alpha)$ in terms of f.)

Solutions

1. By Theorem 7 in Section 5.5 of *Unit 5*, $f^{(n)}$ is analytic on *R*. By inspection of the proof of Theorem 8 there, the integration by parts is valid for any closed contour Γ, so we need only the starting point for the sequence of integrations by parts

$$2\pi i f^{(n)}(\alpha) = \int_\Gamma \frac{f^{(n)}(z)}{z - \alpha}\,dz,$$

which is supplied by Cauchy's Formula in this unit.

2. We have

$$z^4 - 1 = (z^2 - 1)(z^2 + 1) = (z + 1)(z - 1)(z + i)(z - i);$$

thus

$$\frac{1}{z^4 - 1} = \frac{1}{2}\left(\frac{1}{z^2 - 1} - \frac{1}{z^2 + 1}\right)$$

$$= -\frac{1}{4}\frac{1}{z + 1} + \frac{1}{4}\frac{1}{z - 1} + \frac{1}{4i}\frac{1}{z + i} - \frac{1}{4i}\frac{1}{z - i}.$$

Hence

$$\int_C \frac{e^z}{z^4 - 1}\,dz = -\frac{1}{4}\int_C \frac{e^z}{z + 1}\,dz + \frac{1}{4}\int_C \frac{e^z}{z - 1}\,dz + \frac{1}{4i}\int_C \frac{e^z}{z + i}\,dz$$

$$-\frac{1}{4i}\int_C \frac{e^z}{z - i}\,dz.$$

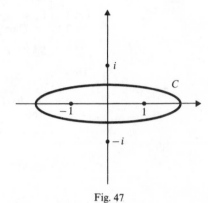

Fig. 47

(i) Thus

$$\int_C \frac{e^z}{z^4 - 1}\,dz = -\frac{1}{4}\cdot 2\pi i e^{-1} + \frac{1}{4}\cdot 2\pi i \cdot e^1 + 0 + 0,$$

since only 1 and -1 are inside *C* (Fig. 47),

$$= \frac{1}{2}\,\pi i\left(e - \frac{1}{e}\right).$$

(ii) In this case

$$\int_C \frac{e^z}{z^4 - 1}\,dz = 0 + 0 + \frac{1}{4i}\cdot 2\pi i e^{-i} - \frac{1}{4i}\cdot 2\pi i \cdot e^i,$$

since only i and $-i$ are inside *C* (Fig. 48),

$$= -2\pi \cdot \tfrac{1}{4}(e^i - e^{-i})$$

$$= -\pi \sinh i = -\pi i \sin 1.$$

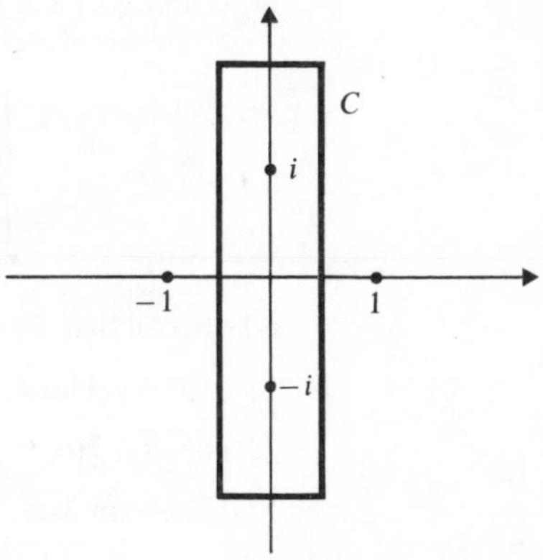

3. (i) Since $g(f(z)) = z$ for all $z \in R_1$,

$$g'(f(z))f'(z) = 1 \quad \text{for all } z \in R_1,$$

and so $g'(f(z)) \neq 0$ for all $z \in R_1$,

that is

$$g'(w) \neq 0 \quad \text{for all } w \in R_2.$$

(ii) $$\int_{g\circ\gamma} h \circ f = \int_a^b (h \circ f)((g \circ \gamma)(t)) \cdot (g \circ \gamma)'(t)\,dt$$

$$= \int_a^b h(f(g(\gamma(t)))) \cdot g'(\gamma(t))\gamma'(t)\,dt$$

$$= \int_a^b h(\gamma(t)) \cdot g'(\gamma(t))\gamma'(t)\,dt, \quad \text{since } f(g(w)) = w,$$

$$= \int_\gamma h(w)g'(w)\,dw$$

$$= \int_\gamma h \cdot g'.$$

(Check carefully the parentheses in line 2 of this solution.)

Fig. 48

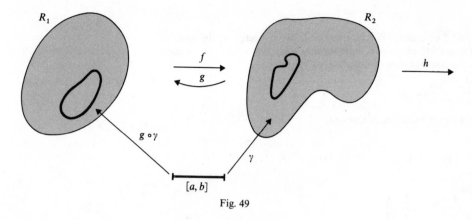

Fig. 49

(iii) Let Γ be a contour in R_2. We must show that

$$\int_{g(\Gamma)} h \circ f = \int_\Gamma h \cdot g'.$$

Let $\Gamma = \Gamma_1 + \cdots + \Gamma_n$ where Γ_r is the path of a smooth arc $\gamma_r : [a_r, b_r] \longrightarrow \mathbf{C}$, $r = 1, \ldots, n$. Then $g \circ \gamma_r$ is a smooth arc with path $g(\Gamma_r)$, and

$$g(\Gamma) = g(\Gamma_1) + \cdots + g(\Gamma_n).$$

Thus

$$\int_{g(\Gamma)} h \circ f = \sum_{r=1}^{n} \int_{g \circ \gamma_r} h \circ f$$

$$= \sum_{r=1}^{n} \int_{\gamma_r} h \cdot g', \quad \text{by (ii)},$$

$$= \int_\Gamma h \cdot g', \quad \text{by definition of } \Gamma.$$

(iv) Let h be analytic on R_2, Γ be a closed contour in R_2. Then $h \circ f$ is analytic on R_1 and $g(\Gamma)$ is a closed contour in R_1; so, by Cauchy's Theorem for the simply-connected region R_1,

$$0 = \int_{g(\Gamma)} h \circ f$$

$$= \int_\Gamma h \cdot g', \quad \text{by (iii)}.$$

(v) Recall that R_2 is Cauchy if $\int_\Gamma h = 0$ for all h analytic on R_2 and closed contours Γ in R_2. Pick such h and Γ. Then by (i) and analyticity of derivatives, h/g' is analytic on R_2. Hence by (iv) *applied to* h/g', $\int_\Gamma \dfrac{h}{g'} \cdot g' = 0$, that is $\int_\Gamma h = 0$, and so, by Theorem 6, R_2 is simply-connected.

4. Any annular sector can be obtained from one like R_2 in Fig. 50 by translation and rotation (which preserve simple connectedness). Let R_2 have outer and inner radii r_2 and r_1 and sector angle 2α. Let R_1 be the rectangle $\{(x, y) : \log r_1 < x < \log r_2, -\alpha < y < \alpha\}$. Since R_1 is contained in the fundamental region $\{(x, y) : x \in \mathbf{R} \text{ and } -\pi < y < \pi\}$ of exp, on which exp has Log as inverse, and R_2 lies in the cut plane which is the domain of Log, Problem 3 applies, with $f(z) = \exp z, z \in R_1$, and $g(w) = \text{Log } w, w \in R_2$, and so R_2 is simply-connected.

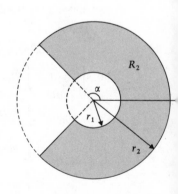

(That translation and rotation do preserve simple-connectedness are obvious geometric facts. You may like to establish these results analytically by using Problem 3 and the facts that translation and rotation are one–one analytic functions.)

5. Introduce line segments joining C_1 to C_2, and let Γ_1 and Γ_2 be the contours shown in the figure.

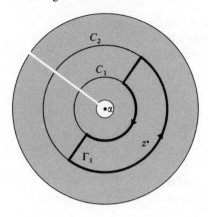 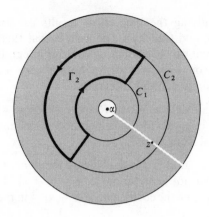

Fig. 51

Now the slit annulus on the left is simply-connected, and so by Theorem 9 (Cauchy's Formula for a simple-closed contour),

$$f(z) = \frac{1}{2\pi i} \int_{\Gamma_1} \frac{f(\zeta)}{\zeta - z}\, d\zeta.$$

Likewise the slit annulus on the right is simply-connected, and so by Cauchy's Theorem,
$\int_{\Gamma_2} \frac{f(\zeta)}{\zeta - z}\, d\zeta = 0$, since $\zeta \longrightarrow \frac{f(\zeta)}{\zeta - z}$ is analytic on the region.

Now $C_2 + (-C_1) = \Gamma_1 + \Gamma_2$ in a suggestive notation; more precisely

$$\frac{1}{2\pi i} \int_{C_2} \frac{f(\zeta)}{\zeta - z}\, d\zeta - \frac{1}{2\pi i} \int_{C_1} \frac{f(\zeta)}{\zeta - z}\, d\zeta = \frac{1}{2\pi i} \int_{\Gamma_1} \frac{f(\zeta)}{\zeta - z}\, d\zeta + \frac{1}{2\pi i} \int_{\Gamma_2} \frac{f(\zeta)}{\zeta - z}\, d\zeta$$

$$= f(z) + 0 = f(z).$$

6. Now $f(\theta) = |\gamma(\theta) - \alpha|$, since $\gamma(\theta) = f(\theta)e^{i\theta} + \alpha$, and $f(\theta) > 0$. Also

$$\text{Wnd}(\gamma, \alpha) = \frac{1}{2\pi i} \int_{\gamma} \frac{dz}{z - \alpha}$$

$$= \frac{1}{2\pi i} \int_0^{2\pi} \frac{\gamma'(\theta)}{\gamma(\theta) - \alpha}\, d\theta.$$

Since $f(\theta) = e^{-i\theta}(\gamma(\theta) - \alpha)$, and γ' exists and is continuous, f' exists and is continuous.

Thus

$$\text{Wnd}(\gamma, \alpha) = \frac{1}{2\pi i} \int_0^{2\pi} \frac{f'(\theta)e^{i\theta} + f(\theta)ie^{i\theta}}{f(\theta)e^{i\theta}}\, d\theta$$

$$= \frac{1}{2\pi i} \int_0^{2\pi} \frac{f'(\theta)}{f(\theta)}\, d\theta + \frac{1}{2\pi} \int_0^{2\pi} 1\, d\theta$$

$$= \frac{1}{2\pi i} \log(f(\theta))\Big|_0^{2\pi} + 1, \quad \text{since } f \text{ is a real function,}$$

$$= 0 + 1, \quad \text{since } f(0) = f(2\pi),$$

$$= 1.$$

A similar result holds for contours.

9.7 THE RESIDUE THEOREM

One good reason for studying the theoretical results on simply-connected regions, winding numbers, and Cauchy's Theorem is that there is a practical payoff: a remarkably efficient way of evaluating contour integrals. The existence of this method is the reason why we did not bother very much with using Cauchy's Formula to evaluate contour integrals.

The method is justified by a result called the *Residue Theorem*, which "reduces" the evaluation of contour integrals to the calculation of residues. So we begin by reviewing some material from *Unit 8*.

Let f have a *singularity* at α—that is, f is analytic on the punctured disc $\{z : 0 < |z - \alpha| < r\}$, for some r, but not analytic on $\{z : |z - \alpha| < r\}$. Then the *residue* $\mathrm{Res}(f, \alpha)$ of f at α is defined to be the coefficient of $(z - \alpha)^{-1}$ in the Laurent series $\sum_{n=-\infty}^{\infty} a_n(z - \alpha)^n$ of f about α—equivalently, $a_{-1} = \dfrac{1}{2\pi i}\displaystyle\int_C f(z)\,dz$ where C is any sufficiently small circle centre α. The *singular part* f_1 of f at α is defined by $f_1(z) = \sum_{n=1}^{\infty} a_{-n}(z - \alpha)^{-n}$—note that f_1 is analytic on the complement of α, and that the residue of f_1 at α is also a_{-1}.

There is a result relating these two notions which is a direct generalization of Theorem 8 on winding number.

Theorem 10

Let f have a singularity at α, with residue a_{-1} and singular part f_1 at α. Let Γ be a simple-closed contour (with positive orientation) not passing through α. Then

$$\frac{1}{2\pi i}\int_\Gamma f_1(z)\,dz = \begin{cases} a_{-1}, & \text{if } \alpha \text{ lies inside } \Gamma \\ 0, & \text{if } \alpha \text{ lies outside } \Gamma. \end{cases}$$

Proof

(1) Let R_1 be the inside of Γ, and suppose that $\alpha \in R_1$. Let C be a small circle centre α such that C and its inside lie in R_1. Proceed as in the proof of Theorem 8 to construct $\Gamma_1, \Gamma_2, \beta$ and M, the curve from "α to ∞".

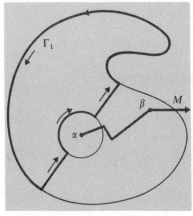

Fig. 52

Since f_1 is analytic on the complement R of M (as $\alpha \in M$), and R is simply-connected, $\displaystyle\int_{\Gamma_1} f_1(z)\,dz = 0$. Similarly, $\displaystyle\int_{\Gamma_2} f_1(z)\,dz = 0$. Thus

$$\int_\Gamma f_1(z)\,dz - \int_C f_1(z)\,dz = \int_{\Gamma_1} f_1(z)\,dz + \int_{\Gamma_2} f_2(z)\,dz = 0,$$

and so

$$\int_\Gamma f_1(z)\, dz = \int_C f_1(z)\, dz$$

$$= 2\pi i a_{-1}, \quad \text{since } a_{-1} \text{ is the residue of } f_1 \text{ at } \alpha.$$

(2)   Let R_2 be the outside of Γ, and suppose that $\alpha \in R_2$. Since R_2 is connected, there is a simple polygonal contour from α to a point β far from Γ, and (as before) we can then add a ray in R_2 from β, as shown in Fig. 53. Let the whole line be called M.

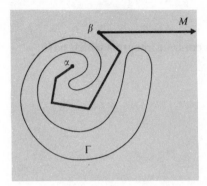

Fig. 53

Then the complement R of M is simply-connected (as in part (1)), and since f_1 is analytic on R, $\int_\Gamma f_1(z)\, dz = 0$. ∎

This theorem is a powerful result. It generalizes Theorem 8, which is obtained by setting $f(z) = \dfrac{1}{z - \alpha}$ (because then $f_1(z) = f(z)$). It also generalizes Cauchy's Formula (Theorem 9) and, in fact, Cauchy's Formula for derivatives. Its only defects for our purposes are the use of f_1 instead of f in the integral, and the restriction to one singularity. Both of these are overcome in the next theorem (which is, like so many others, due to Cauchy).

Theorem 11   (The Residue Theorem)

Let R be a simply-connected region, $\alpha_1, \ldots, \alpha_n$ be points of R, and f be a function analytic on R except for singularities at $\alpha_1, \ldots, \alpha_n$ (so that f is analytic on $R - \{\alpha_1, \ldots, \alpha_n\}$). Let Γ be any simple-closed contour in R not passing through any of $\alpha_1, \ldots, \alpha_n$. Then

$$\int_\Gamma f(z)\, dz = 2\pi i \sum_{j \in S} \text{Res}(f, \alpha_j),$$

where $S = \{j : 1 \leqslant j \leqslant n \text{ and } \alpha_j \text{ lies inside } \Gamma\}$. In other words,

$$\int_\Gamma f(z)\, dz = 2\pi i \times \text{the sum of the residues of } f \text{ at those singularities of}$$

$$f \text{ lying inside } \Gamma.$$

Proof

We consider the function g, which is "f with all its singular parts removed". More precisely, let f_r be the singular part of f at α_r (for $r = 1, \ldots, n$); then f_r is analytic on the set $R - \{\alpha_r\}$. Let $g(z) = f(z) - \sum_{r=1}^{n} f_r(z)$. Then g is analytic on $R - \{\alpha_1, \ldots, \alpha_n\}$ but has singularities at each α_r. However, by Theorem 1 of *Unit 8*, $f - f_r$ has a removable singularity at α_r, and so g does (since $f_1, \ldots, f_{r-1}, f_{r+1}, \ldots, f_n$ are all analytic on neighbourhoods of α_r). Remove the singularities of g at $\alpha_1, \ldots, \alpha_n$: then g is analytic on R. Thus by Cauchy's Theorem, $\int_\Gamma g(z)\,dz = 0$. But since none of $\alpha_1, \ldots, \alpha_n$ lie on Γ we can rearrange this to say that

$$\int_\Gamma \left(f(z) - \sum_{r=1}^n f_r(z) \right) dz = 0,$$

that is

$$\int_\Gamma f(z)\,dz = \sum_{r=1}^n \int_\Gamma f_r(z)\,dz.$$

The result follows by applying Theorem 10. ∎

Let us now apply Theorem 11 to evaluate certain contour integrals which have cropped up previously.

Example 1 (Example 2 of Section 9.5)

Evaluate $\displaystyle\int_C \frac{\sin z}{z^2 - 1}\,dz$, where C is

(i)   the ellipse $x^2 + 4y^2 = 4$,

(ii)   the square with vertices $\pm\frac{1}{2} \pm \frac{1}{2}i$.

Solution

The function $f(z) = \dfrac{\sin z}{z^2 - 1}$ has singularities at 1 and -1: that at 1 is a simple pole with residue $\dfrac{\sin 1}{2} = \frac{1}{2}\sin 1$, and that at -1 is a simple pole with residue $\dfrac{\sin(-1)}{-2} = \frac{1}{2}\sin 1$ (both these calculations follow from the Result on page 51 of *Unit 8*).

(i)   Since -1 and 1 both lie inside C,

$$\int_C f = 2\pi i(\tfrac{1}{2}\sin 1 + \tfrac{1}{2}\sin 1) = 2\pi i \sin 1.$$

(ii)   Since -1 and 1 both lie outside C,

$$\int_C f = 2\pi i \cdot 0 = 0.$$

Example 2 (based on Example 2 of Section 5.5 of *Unit 5*)

What are the possible values of $\displaystyle\int_\Gamma \frac{\sin z}{z^4}\,dz$ where Γ is a simple-closed contour not passing through 0?

Solution

Let $f(z) = \dfrac{\sin z}{z^4}$. Now f has a pole at 0, and since

$$\frac{\sin z}{z^4} = z^{-3} - \frac{1}{6}z^{-1} + \frac{1}{5!}z - \cdots,$$

the residue of f at 0 is $-\frac{1}{6}$. Thus $\displaystyle\int_\Gamma f = 2\pi i \cdot (-\frac{1}{6}) = -\frac{1}{3}\pi i$, if 0 lies inside Γ, while $\displaystyle\int_\Gamma f = 0$ if 0 lies outside Γ.

In the next unit we shall show how the Residue Theorem can be used to evaluate many real integrals, and to sum series, by transforming them into contour integrals. You will see that the Residue Theorem, although using very theoretical concepts in its statement, is a tool of great practical power. But since it requires a facility with calculating residues in order to be useful, we shall not set any problems on it in this unit.

Summary

In this section we have proved the Residue Theorem, and mentioned its usefulness in evaluating contour integrals.

Self-Assessment Questions

1. State the Residue Theorem.

2. Use the Residue Theorem to evaluate $\int_\Gamma \dfrac{\cos z}{z} \, dz$ where Γ is any ellipse enclosing the origin.

Solutions

1. See Theorem 11 on page 103.

2. Since $z \longrightarrow \dfrac{\cos z}{z}$ has a simple pole at 0 with residue $\cos 0 = 1$, and 0 lies inside Γ, $\int_\Gamma \dfrac{\cos z}{z} \, dz = 2\pi i$.

NOTATION

The following items of notation are explained on the pages given. Most other items of notation used in the text may be found in one of the following: *Mathematical Handbook* for M100, The Mathematics Foundation Course; *Handbook* for M231, Analysis; *Units 1, 2, 3, 4, 5 and 6* of M332, Complex Analysis.

cosec   10

tan   16

$\lim_{z \to \alpha} f(z) = \infty$ 21

cot   34

$\lim_{z \to \infty} f(z) = 0$ 34

$\sum_{n=-\infty}^{\infty} a_n(z - \alpha)^n$ 38

$\text{Res}(f, \alpha)$ 50

$\text{Wnd}(\Gamma, \alpha)$ 84

$\pm a \pm bi$ 92

$f_1(z) = \sum_{n=1}^{\infty} a_{-n}(z - \alpha)^{-n}$ 102

INDEX

COMPLEX ANALYSIS

Course Team

Chairman:	Dr. G. A. Read	Senior Lecturer
Authors:	Dr. P. D. Bacsich	Lecturer
	Dr. M. Crampin	Lecturer
	Mr. N. W. Gowar	Senior Lecturer
	Dr. R. J. Wilson	Lecturer
Editor:	Mr. R. J. Knight	Lecturer
B.B.C.:	Mr. D. Saunders	

With assistance from:

Mr. R. Clamp	B.B.C.
Mr. D. Goldrei	Course Assistant
Mr. H. Hoggan	B.B.C.
Mr. R. J. Margolis	Staff Tutor
Dr. A. R. Meetham	Staff Tutor
Mr. J. E. Phythian	Staff Tutor
Mr. J. Richmond	B.B.C.
Mrs. P. M. Shepheard Rogers	Course Assistant
Dr. C. A. Rowley	Course Assistant